ESTATE PUBLICATIONS

'UNBRIDGE WELLS · TON
ROWBOROUGH · PADDOCK WOOD

G000143809

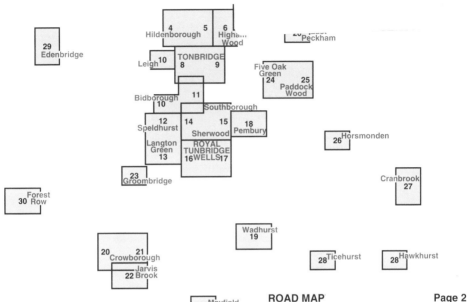

ROAD MAP — Page 2
ROYAL TUNBRIDGE WELLS
ENLARGED CENTRE — Page 3
INDEX TO STREETS — Page 31

Scale of street plans: 4 Inches to 1 Mile (unless otherwise stated)

▬▬ Motorway		∿ Stream / River
'A' Road / Dual		Canal (Lock)
'B' Road / Dual		→ One-way Street
Minor Road / Dual		🅿 Car Park
▬▬ Track		🅲 Public Convenience
▨ Pedestrianized		🅸 Tourist Information
▬■▬ Railway / Station		✛ Place of Worship
- - - Footpath		● Post Office

Every effort has been made to verify the accuracy of information in this book but the publishers cannot accept responsibility for expense or loss caused by an error or omission. Information that will be of assistance to the user of the maps will be welcomed.

The representation on these maps of a road, track or path is no evidence of the existence of a right of way.

Street plans prepared and published by ESTATE PUBLICATIONS, Bridewell House, TENTERDEN, KENT.
The Publishers acknowledge the co-operation of the local authorities
of towns represented in this atlas.

Ordnance Survey® This product includes mapping data licensed from Ordnance Survey®
with the permission of the Controller of Her Majesty's Stationery Office.

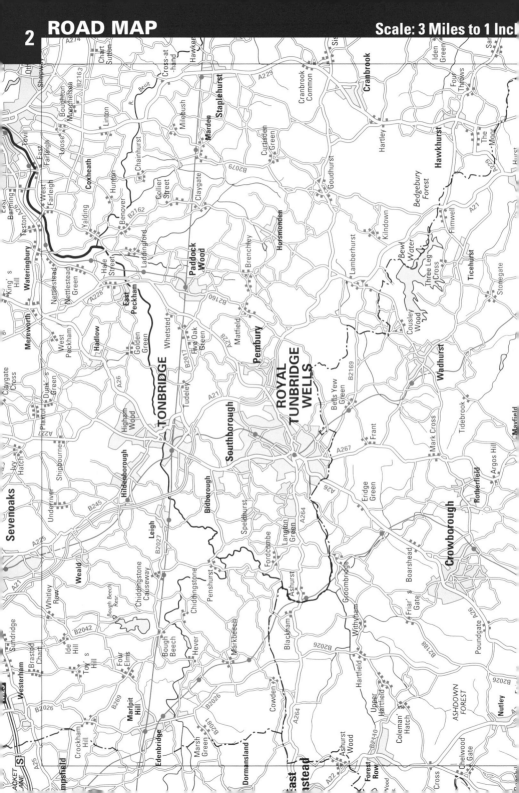

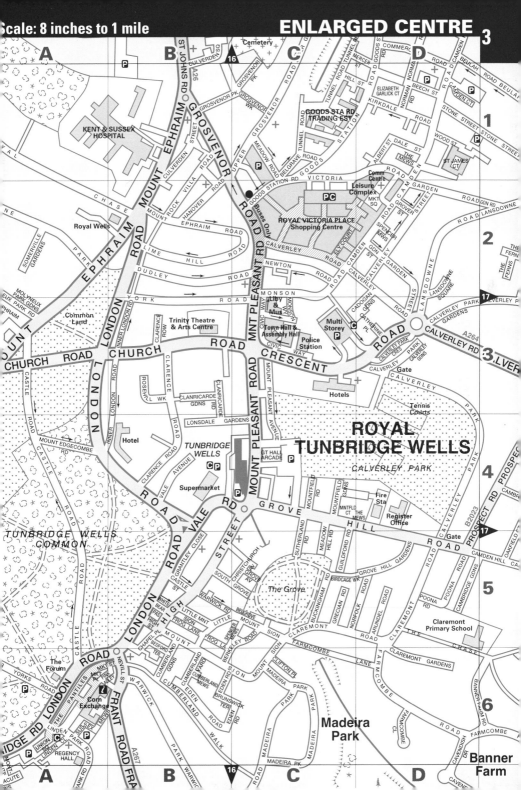

ROYAL TUNBRIDGE WELLS

HILDENBOROUGH

4

A — B — C — D

Oakhurst Wood

Cock Wood

1

HILDENBROOK FARM

LANE

RIDING LANE

MILL LANE

VINES LANE

ROAD LONDON

B245

GARLANDS

2

The Limes Farm

MILL LANE

Great Forge Farm

Hollanden Park Farm

Watt's Cross

RIDING LANE

St Michaels Ct

Raphael Medical Centre

Raphael Ct

Sch

3

A21

Oak Tree Farm

Flat Wood

Red Ground

RIDING PK

HARDWICK RD

Derby Cl

Harbour

WATTS CROSS ROAD

FOXBUSH

Sch

P

Liby

MNT PLEASANT CT

MOUNT PLEASANT

KNOWSLEY

Mnt Pleasant Rd

Derby Cl

NOBLE

TREE ROAD

TONBRIDGE ROAD

CHURCH RD

WAY

PHILPOTS LANE

POTS LANE

HAZELS LANE

4

TONBRIDGE

Sch

WEALD CT

MOON

FRANCIS RD

OLD HARBOUR

Oakhill House Fidelity

HILDENBOROUGH

Hildenborough Medical Centre

West Wood

LEIGH ROAD

WOODFIELD AV

5

Lucy's Farm

STREET LOWER

Club House

Golf Course

RINGS HILL STREET

STOCKS GREEN ROAD

STOCKS GREEN ROAD

FELLOWES

WILSON CL

School

FIR TREE CL

MEAD

WEALDE

6

B2027

RINGS HILL

BY-PASS

ROAD

TONB

A21

STOCKS GREEN

Stocks Green

STOCKS GREEN ROAD

LEIGH ROAD

LEIGH ROAD

BROOKMEAD

BIRCH CL

GREENVIEW CRESCENT

ASHLEY ROAD

COPSE RD

BYRNE

Selbys Farm

Hilden Park

A — B — **8** — C — D

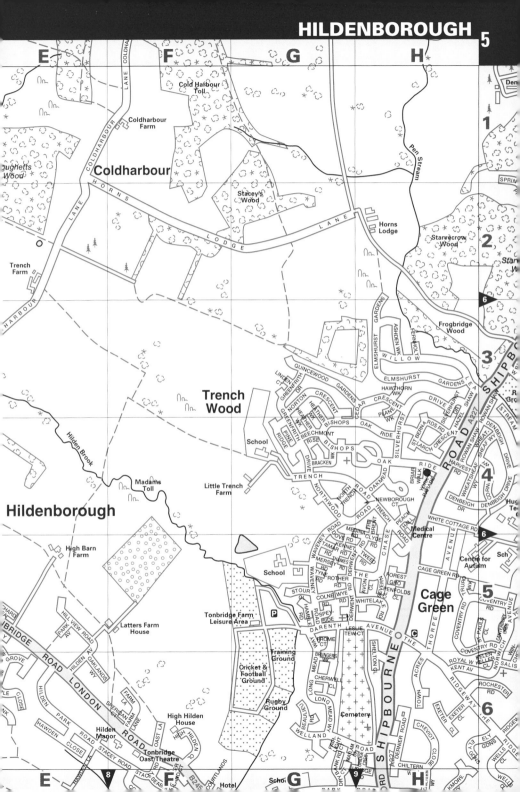

E   **F**   **G**   **H**

Cold Harbour Toll

Coldharbour Farm

Coldharbour

Stacey's Wood

Jughetts Wood

HORNS LANE

COLDHARBOUR LANE

LODGE LANE

Pen Stream

Horns Lodge

Starvecrow Wood

Star W

SPRIN

1

2

Trench Farm

Frogbridge Wood

3

Trench Wood

ELMSHURST GARDENS

ASHDEN WK

FERN HOLT

WILLOW

ELMSHURST GARDENS

HAWTHORN WK

QUINCEWOOD GARDENS

LINDEN CL

GREENFRITH DR

NORTON CRESCENT

HEATHER RISE

PINE RIDGE

BISHOPS

CEDAR CRESCENT

PLANE WK

HAZEL RD

SILVERHURST

ST BERNA RDS RD

ROWAN SHAW

SILVERHURST DRIVE

SHIPBO

SHIPBOURNE ROAD A227

R Gro

R STREAM

Hilden Brook

School

Madams Toll

Little Trench Farm

BEECHMONT

BISHOPS

BRACKEN

OAK

GREENFRITH DRIVE

TRENCH DRIVE

NORTHWOOD ROAD

NORTH TRENCH ROAD

OAK RIDE

OAKMEAD

SILVERHURST

BRIAR WALK

RIDE

HARVESHEAP

WHEATSHEAF

DENBEIGH DR

DENBEIGH

SHEAF WY

4

Hildenborough

High Barn Farm

NEWBOROUGH CT

PEACH

WHITE COTTAGE RD

Medical Centre

Hug Te

Sch

Centre for Autism

5

Cage Green

BRENT

TRENCH ROAD

CLYDE

MEDINA RD

DOVE RD

KENNET RD

TAMAR RD

TWEED

THAMES

CHASE

AVENUE

FOREST GRO

CAGE GREEN RP

COVENTRY RD

TRURO WY

ST PAULS

COVENTRY RD

KENT AV

ROYAL W

HELEN KELLER CL

N SALIS

ROCHESTER RD

School

Tonbridge Farm Leisure Area

WAVENEY ROAD

MERSEY RD

TYNE RD

ROTHER RD

STOUR CL

COLNE RD

HAMBLE LYN

DERWENT

RENFOLDS CL

WHITELAK RD

AVON CL

THORPE AVENUE

LESLIE TEW CT

SHELTON

ACRES

TOWN

EXETER RD

ELY GDNS

RIDGE

6

Latters Farm House

Training Ground

Cricket & Football Ground

Rugby Ground

Cemetery

High Hilden House

Hilden Manor

Tonbridge Oast Theatre

CHERWELL CL

BRUNGERS WK

LONG MEAD WY

BEAULIEU RD

WELLAND

DARENTH RD

FROME

MEAD

MATAM ROAD

DERNIER ROAD

CHILTERN

CHEVIOT CL

RIDGEWAY CL

KMORE

WELLS

HILL VIEW ROAD

PARK AV

OAKLANDS WY

HILDEN PARK ROAD

FARM CL

SHERIDAN

OAST LA

HIGH HILDEN CL

STACEY ROAD

STACEY SEAL

B245

HAWDEN

CLOSE

LONDON ROAD

BRIDGE ROAD

GROVE

HARDW

PARK AV

HILTON

Hotel

School

SHIPBOURNE ROAD

E   **8**   **F**   **G**   **9**   **H**

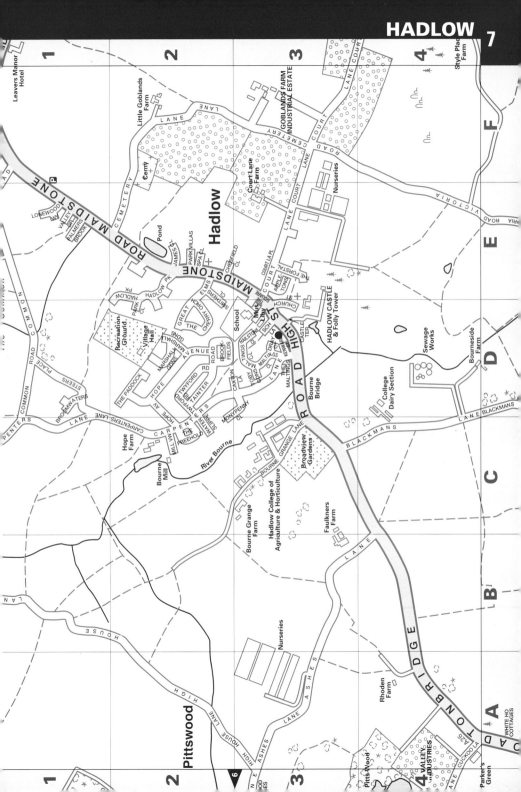

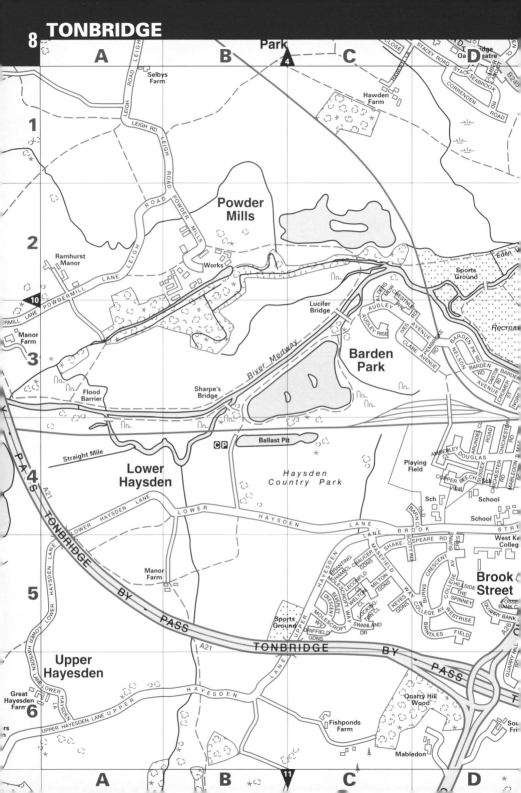

A   **B**   Park   **C**   **D**

Selbys Farm

Hawden Farm

Stacey Road

Oa

dge Teatre

STACE

SEABROOK

CORRENDEN ROAD

B245

1

LEIGH ROAD

LEIGH RD

LEIGH ROAD

POWDER MILLS

Powder Mills

2

Ramhurst Manor

LEIGH LANE

Works

Eden

Sports Ground

Recrea

POWDERMILL LANE

10

Lucifer Bridge

ALDERS MDW

CHESTNUT MW

AUDLEY AVE

IVES AVENUE

CAMBROKE RD

NELSON

BARDEN PK RD

BARDEN RD

CASTOR RD

CROMER RD

BARDEN NORT

RMILL LANE

Manor Farm

3

River Medway

Sharpe's Bridge

AUDLEY RISE

CLARE AVENUE

Barden Park

BARDEN AVENUE

Flood Barrier

C P

Ballast Pit

ARUNDEL ROAD

DOUGLAS

CHICHESTER RD

Straight Mile

4

A21

TONBRIDGE

Lower Haysden

LOWER HAYSDEN LANE

LOWER HAYSDEN LANE

Haysden Country Park

Playing Field

AMBERLEY CL

SUSSEX

COPPER BEECH

VIEW

Sch

Sch

School

School

STRE

LOWER HAYSDEN LANE

BROOK

West Ke Colleg

Brook Street

5

BY - PASS

Manor Farm

Sports Ground

HAYESDEN LANE

BRANTING-HAM CL

MOLESCROFT WAY

LECONFIELD

SHAKE-SPEARE RD

SCOTT RD

MAYFIELD

MILTON GDNS

KEYES GDNS

WAY

BURNS CRESCENT

COLLEGE AV

COLLEGE AV

HILLSIDE

THE SPINNEY

WESTRISE

FOSSE BANK C

QUARRY BANK

BEVERLEY CRES

WELTON CL

LOCKING

TOT CL

SWANLAND DR

DRIFFIELD GDNS

MOLESCROFT WY

BRINDLES

FIELD

A21

Upper Hayesden

TONBRIDGE BY - PASS

T

6

Great Hayesden Farm

LOWER HAYSDEN LANE

LOWER HAYSDEN LA

HAYESDEN LANE

UPPER HAYESDEN LANE UPPER

UPPER HAYESDEN

Fishponds Farm

Quarry Hill Wood

QUARRY HILL

Sou Fri

Mabledon

rs

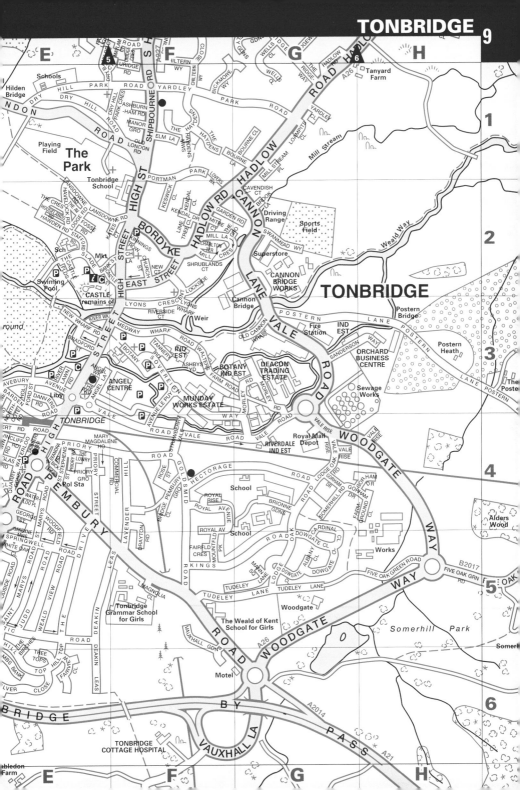

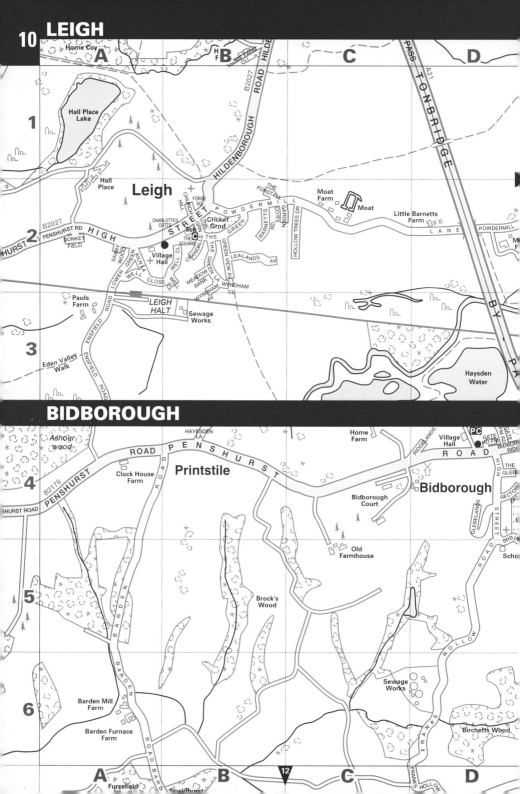

A   B   C   D

Home Cov

H F

HOME FARM CL

B2027

HILDENBOROUGH ROAD

HILDE

PASS

TON-BRIDGE

A21

1

Hall Place Lake

Hall Place

Leigh

HILDENBOROUGH ROAD

THE FORSTAL

Moat Farm

Moat

Little Barnetts Farm

HURST

2

B2027

PENSHURST RD

HIGH

DONKEY FIELD

CHURCH
SQ

FORGE
SQ

HILL

CHURCH GREEN

STREET

Sch

Cricket Grnd

POWDERMILL

GREEN

BARNETTS CL

RD

GARDEN CL

HOLLOW TREES DR

THE
COTTS

LANE

POWDERMILL

M F

CHARLOTTES
COTTS

THE SQUARE

CHANDLERS

SAXBY
WOOD

KILN LA

LOWER GREEN

WELL CLOSE

WELL

WELL CL

THE GREEN

GREEN LA

MEADOW BANK

GREEN VIEW AV

WYNDHAM AV

WYNDHAM CL

LEALANDS AV

Village Hall

3

Pauls Farm

ENSFIELD

ROAD

LEIGH HALT

Sewage Works

BY

PA

Eden Valley Walk

ENSFIELD

ROAD

Haysden Water

A   B   C   D

4

Ashour Wood

HAYESDEN LA

PENSHURST

ROAD

ROAD

PENSHURST

Printstile

Home Farm

RIDGELANDS

Village Hall

PC

ROAD

GATE HO FM RD

BIDBOR
RIDG

B2176

PENSHURST

ROAD

Clock House Farm

Bidborough Court

Bidborough

HIGH

THE GLEBE

RECTOR

SHURST ROAD

GLEBELANDS

STREET

Sch

ROAD

SPR

Old Farmhouse

5

BARDEN

Brock's Wood

HOLLOW

Sewage Works

6

Barden Mill Farm

BARDEN

Barden Furnace Farm

ROAD BARD

FRANKS

Birchetts Wood

A

Furzefield

B

Shellhurst

12

FRANKS

HOLLOW

C

D

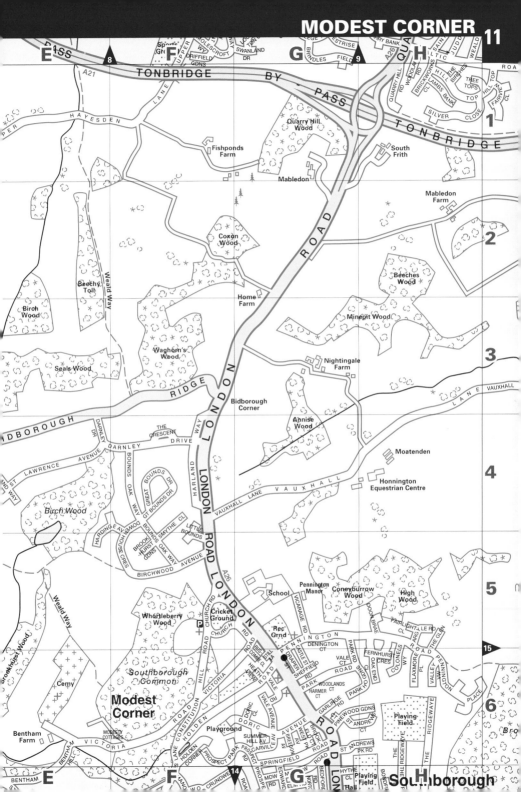

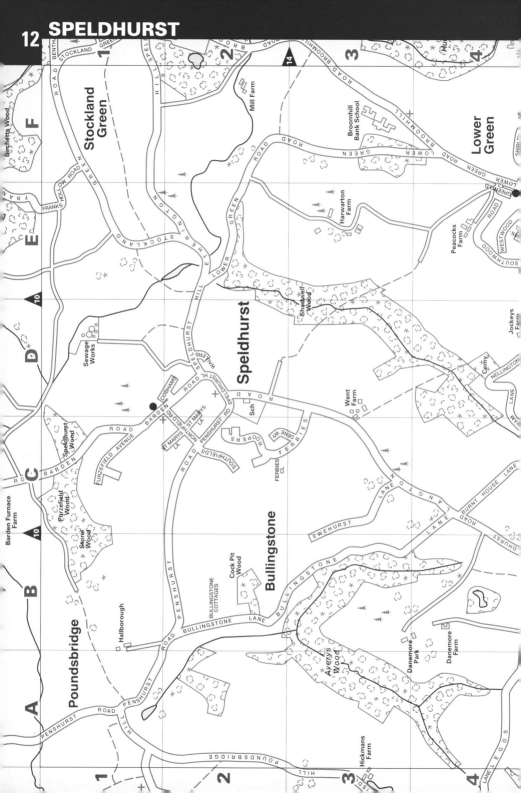

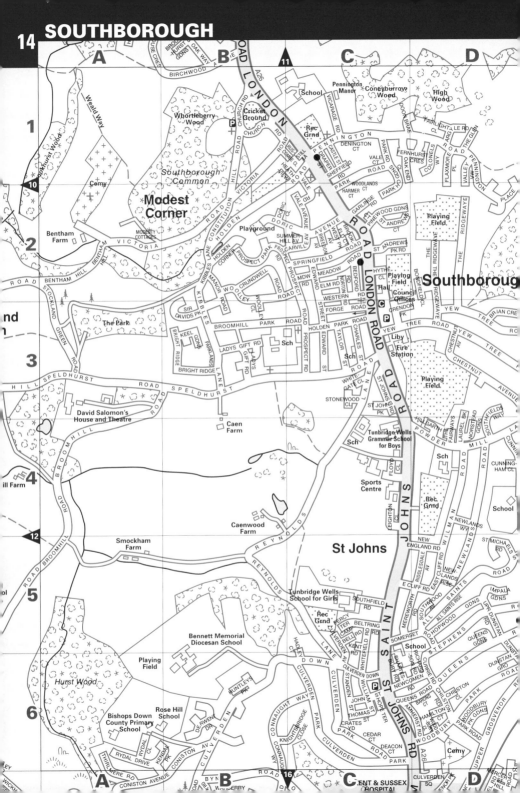

SOUTHBOROUGH

14

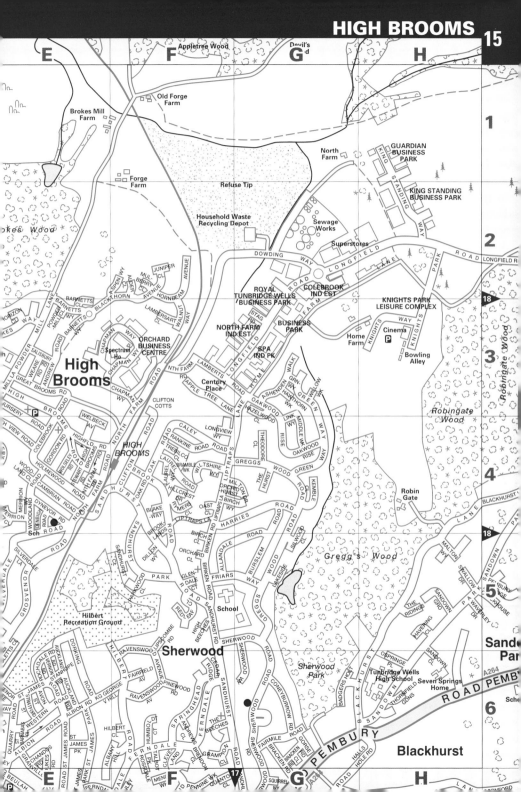

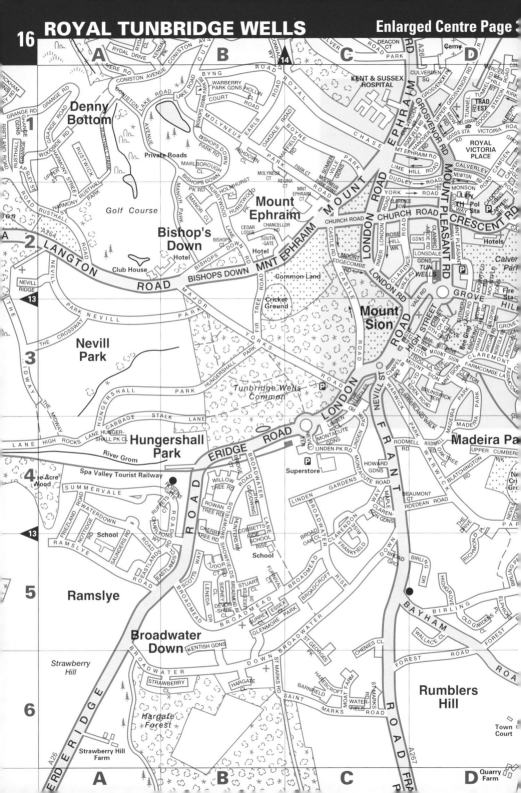

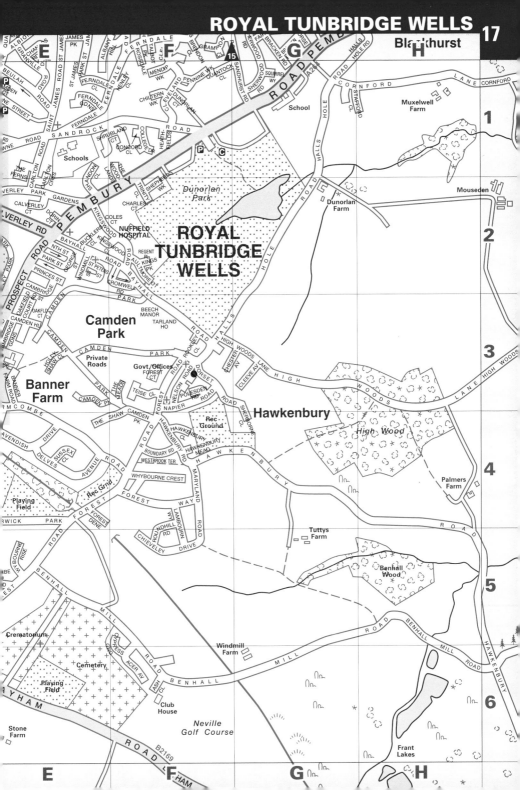

Blackhurst

ROYAL TUNBRIDGE WELLS

Dunorlan Park

Camden Park

Banner Farm

Hawkenbury

High Wood

Muxelwell Farm

Mouseden

Dunorlan Farm

Palmers Farm

Tuttys Farm

Benhall Wood

Crematorium

Cemetery

Playing Field

Windmill Farm

Club House

Neville Golf Course

Stone Farm

Frant Lakes

Private Roads

Rec Ground

Govt. Offices

Playing Field

School

Schools

Nuffield Hospital

Beech Manor

Tarland Ho

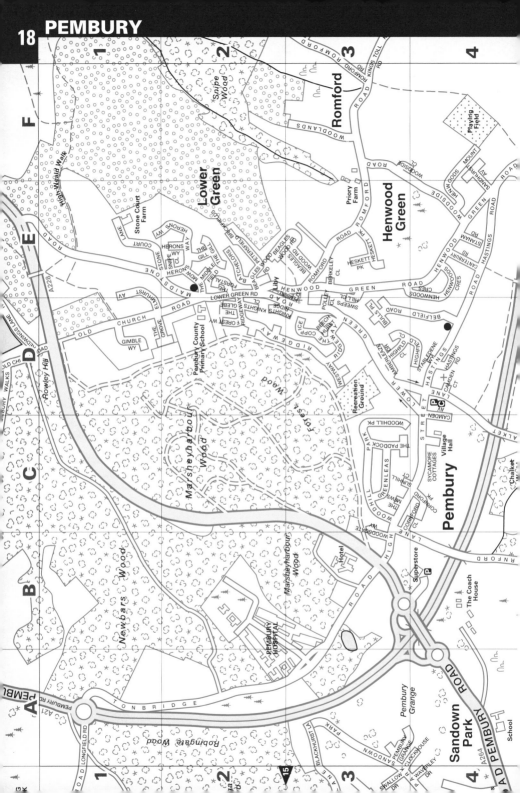

Romford

Lower Green

Henwood Green

Pembury

Snipe Wood

Priory Farm

Stone Court Farm

High Weald Walk

Heronswharf

Marsheyharbour Wood

Newbars Wood

Forest Wood

Robingate Wood

Pembury County Primary School

Recreation Ground

PEMBURY HOSPITAL

Hotel

Superstore

The Coach House

Village Hall

Sandown Park

Pembury Grange

Tonbridge

Playing Field

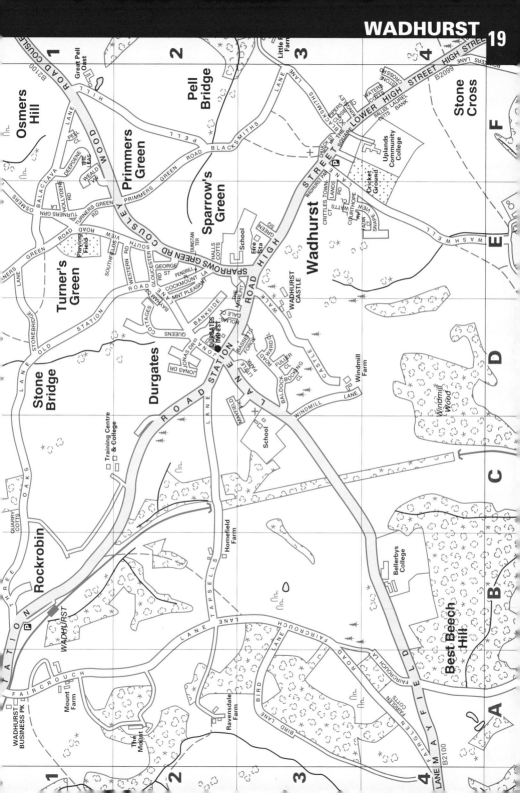

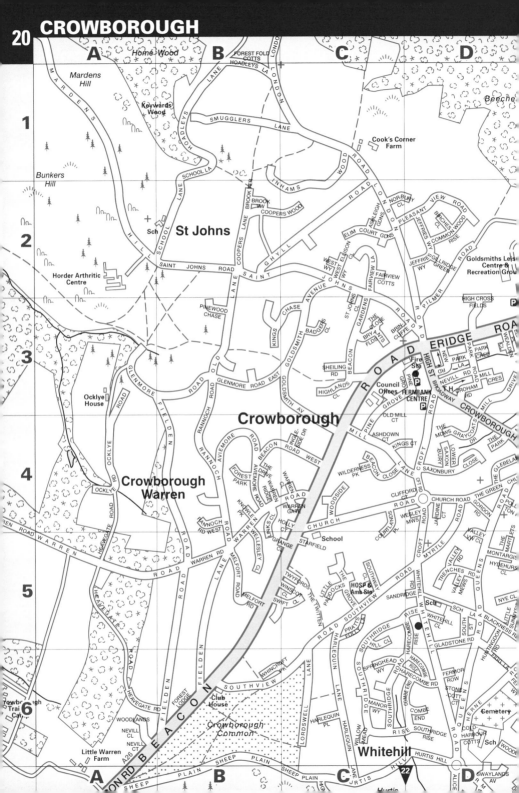

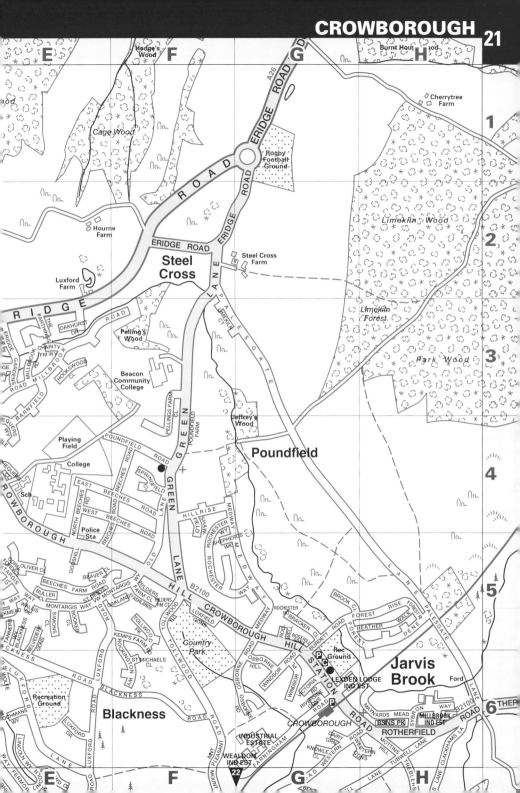

Map legend labels:

E **F** **G** **H**

Hodge's Wood

Burnt Houn Wood

Cherrytree Farm

ERIDGE ROAD A26

Cage Wood

Rogby Football Ground

1

Limekiln Wood

Hourne Farm

ERIDGE ROAD

2

Steel Cross

Steel Cross Farm

Luxford Farm

Limekiln Forest

LANE

PALESGATE

ERIDGE ROAD

THE FARTHINGS

OAKHURST DR

Pelling's Wood

Park Wood

3

RIDGE

ERIDGE GARDENS

MILLBROOK

CHARITY FM WY

HOOKSWOOD CL

Beacon Community College

Pellings Farm

Poundfield Farm

Jeffrey's Wood

Poundfield

BARNFIELD

Playing Field

POUNDFIELD ROAD

GREEN LANE

College

SPRINGFIELD CL

HILLRISE

4

Sch

ROWBOROUGH

EAST BEECHES RD

NORTH BEECHES

WEST BEECHES

BEECHES ROAD

BEECHES ROAD

OLD LANE

ROCHESTER CL

MEDWAY

SHEPHERDS WK

MYTH

Police Sta

DOGSHILL

BEAVER FL

HILL CROWBOROUGH

B2100

ROCHESTER

MEDWAY

BROOK LA

RISE

FOREST

WALK

DENE

5

OLIVER CL

BEECHES FARM ROAD

ST PETERS

WILDERS FARM CL

HOLDERS FM WY

LOXFIELD GDNS

ROCHESTER

HOBRACKEN

ROSEHILL

BURDETT ROAD

FOREST RISE

HEATHER

PALESGATE

MONTARGIS WAY

BULLER

OAKLANDS

ASHLANDS

TOLLWOOD RD

Country Park

OSBORNE HILL

WINDSOR

VICTORIA RD

ROSEHILL

Rec Ground

FOREST DENE

HELVEDERE CL

KEMPS FARM L

ROCKINGTON CL

ST MICHAELS CL

BLACKNESS

Recreation Ground

LUXFORD ROAD

WINDSOR RD

OSBORNE

STATION ROAD

LEXDEN LODGE IND EST

Jarvis Brook

Ford

6

THER

LINCOLN WY

LUXFORD DR

Blackness

FARNINGHAM

CROWBOROUGH

RIVERSIDE GDNS

DAIRY GRN

KNOWLE CL

ROTHERFIELD

MAYNARDS MEAD

MILLBROOK IND EST

BSNS PK

MOTTINS HILL

WESTERN ROAD

TUBWELL LANE

CLACKHAMS LA

TREBLE

INDUSTRIAL ESTATE

WEALDON IND EST

22

E **F** **G** **H**

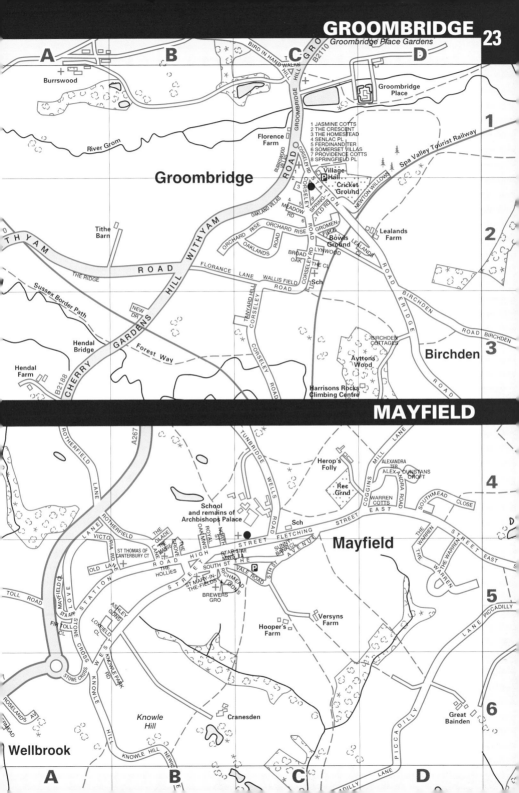

Groombridge Place Gardens

Burrswood

River Grom

Florence Farm

Groombridge Place

1 JASMINE COTTS
2 THE CRESCENT
3 THE HOMESTEAD
4 SENLAC PL
5 FERDINAND TER
6 SOMERSET VILLAS
7 PROVIDENCE COTTS
8 SPRINGFIELD PL

Spa Valley Tourist Railway

Village Hall

Cricket Ground

Groombridge

Tithe Barn

Lealands Farm

Bowls Ground

THYAM

ROAD WITHYAM

THE RIDGE

Orchard Rise

Oaklands

Broad Oak

Lynwood

Birchden

Sussex Border Path

Hendal Bridge

Forest Way

Ayttons Wood

Birchden Cottages

Hendal Farm

Harrisons Rocks Climbing Centre

Herop's Folly

Alexandra Ter

Dunstans Croft

School and remains of Archbishops Palace

Rec Grnd

Warren Cotts

Mayfield

St Thomas of Canterbury CT

Old Lane

St Mary-in-the-Fields

Brewers Gro

Versyns Farm

Hooper's Farm

Toll Road

Knowle Hill

Cranesden

Great Bainden

Wellbrook

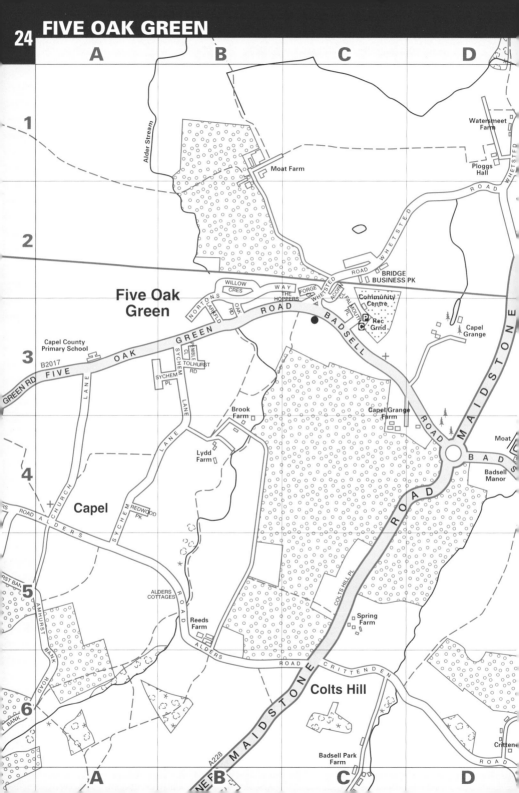

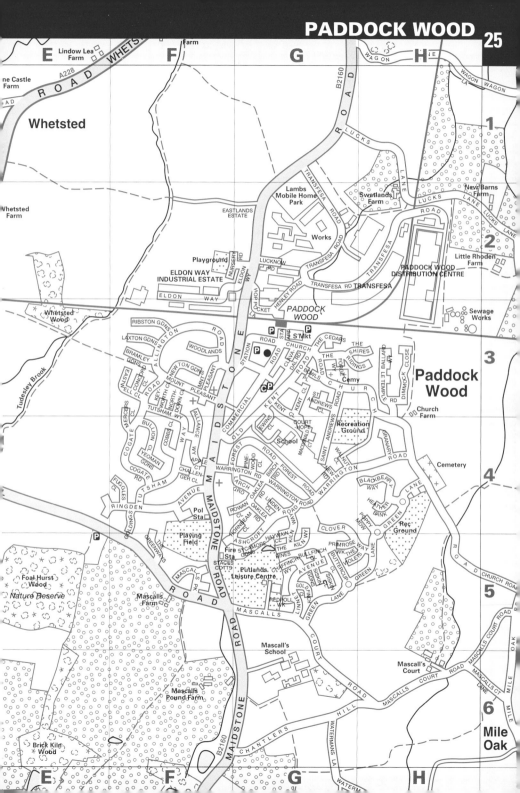

Whetsted

Lindow Lea Farm

Farm

ne Castle Farm

ROAD WHETSTED

Whetsted Farm

Whetsted Wood

Tudesley Brook

EASTLANDS ESTATE

Playground

ELDON WAY INDUSTRIAL ESTATE

Lambs Mobile Home Park

Works

NURSERY RD

LUCKNOW RD

ELDON WY

HOP POCKET LA

ELDON WAY

HENLEY ROAD

TRANSFESA ROAD

TRANSFESA RD

PADDOCK WOOD

TRANSFESA

Swatlands Farm

LUCKS LANE

New Barns Farm

LA

LUCKS ROAD

Little Rhoden Farm

PADDOCK WOOD DISTRIBUTION CENTRE

Sewage Works

WAGON

WAGON LA

WAGON

B2160 ROAD LUCKS LANE

RIBSTON GDNS

LAXTON GDNS

BRAMLEY GDNS

EASNELL CL

CONGATE CL

COGATE MERCERS CL

BULLION CL

YEOMAN

COGATE GDNS

FUGGLES CL

TUTSHAM

Ringden

WOODLANDS

ALLINGTON ROAD

NEWTON GDNS

WORTH NORTH WY

MOUNT PLEASANT

KEY

TUTSHAM RD

COBBS CL

CHALLENGER CL

APPLE CT

AVENUE

THE GREENWAYS

MAIDSTONE ROAD

STATION ROAD

COMMERCIAL ROAD

FOREST ROAD

S'Mkt

CHURCH ROAD

CLAVA DA RD

BOWLS

KENT CL

KENT CL

JEWINS CL

COURT HOPE

MACDONALD

School

PINE WOOD

LINDEN RD

LARCH GRO

ROWAN CL

HORNBEAM CL

ASHCROFT

SYCAMORE GDNS

HAYWAIN

PINES

STAGES COTTS

Fire Sta

THE CEDARS

THE SHIRES

THE RIDINGS

FORGE CL

THE FORGE

ANDREWS RD

SAINT ANDREWS CL

SAINT ANDREWS

WARRINGTON RD

BIRCH FOREST ROAD

OAKLEA

KILN WY

CHAFFINCH

BULLFINCH

Cemy

Recreation Ground

WANTON

WARRINGTON ROAD

BLACKBERRY WAY

HEATHER BANK

PRIMROSE WAY

CLOVER

GREEN LANE

THE MOLEYS

POPPY MDW

PUTLANDS

Paddock Wood

LE TEMPLE

BALLARD WY

DIMMOCK CLOSE

CHURCH ROAD

GRANARY ROAD

Church Farm

Cemetery

Rec Ground

FOREST ROAD

Foal Hurst Wood

Nature Reserve

STAGES PK

MASCALLS RD

Mascalls Farm

Mascall's School

Mascalls Pound Farm

Brick Kiln Wood

Putlands Leisure Centre

REDHOLT WK

GOLDFINCH

LINNET

SISKIN

SISKIN

KILN AVENUE

BUTTERCUP

GREEN LANE

COURT ROAD

MASCALLS

B2160 MAIDSTONE ROAD

CHANTLERS

HILL

WATERMANS LA

WATERMAN

Mascall's Court

MASCALLS COURT ROAD

MASCALLS CT LANE

MILE OAK ROAD

CHURCH ROAD

Mile Oak

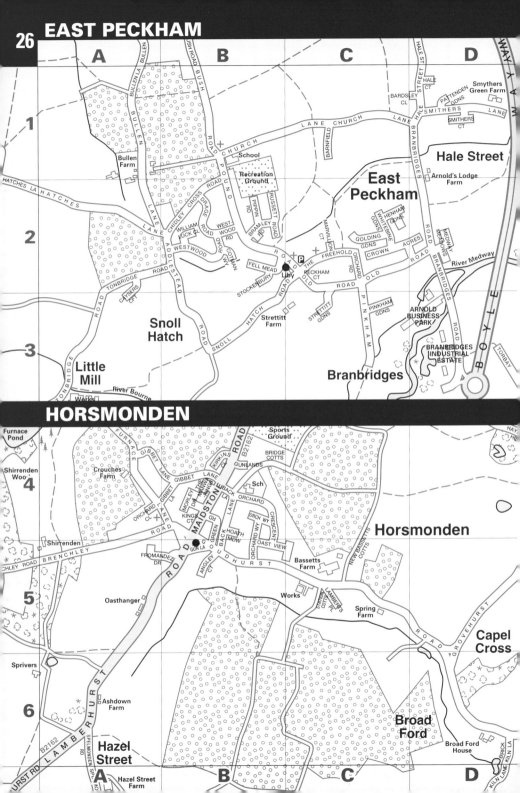

A B C D

1

2

3

Hale Street

East Peckham

Arnold's Lodge Farm

Snoll Hatch

Little Mill

Branbridges

Bullen Farm

School

Recreation Ground

Strettitt Farm

River Bourne

River Medway

ARNOLD BUSINESS PARK

BRANBRIDGES INDUSTRIAL ESTATE

Smythers Green Farm

HORSMONDEN

A B C D

4

5

6

Horsmonden

Capel Cross

Broad Ford

Hazel Street

Furnace Pond

Shirrenden Wood

Crouches Farm

Shirrenden

Oasthanger

Sprivers

Ashdown Farm

Sports Ground

Bridge Cotts

Sch

Bassetts Farm

Works

Spring Farm

New Bassetts Cotts

Hazel Street Farm

Broad Ford House

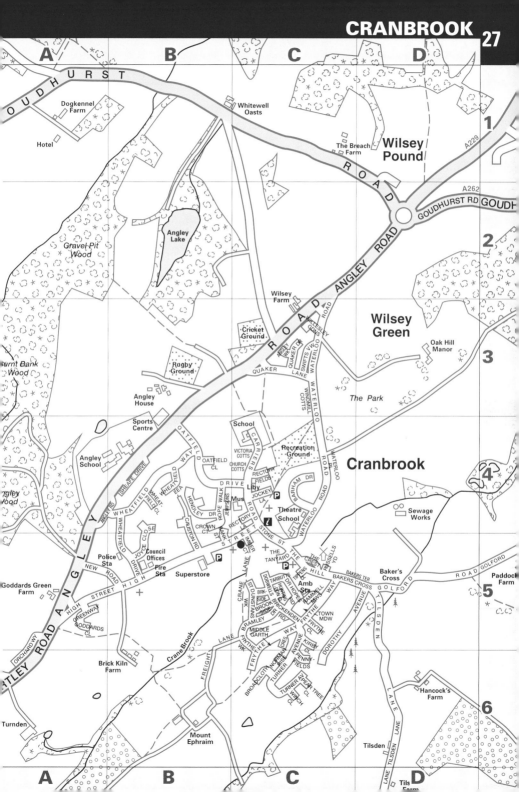

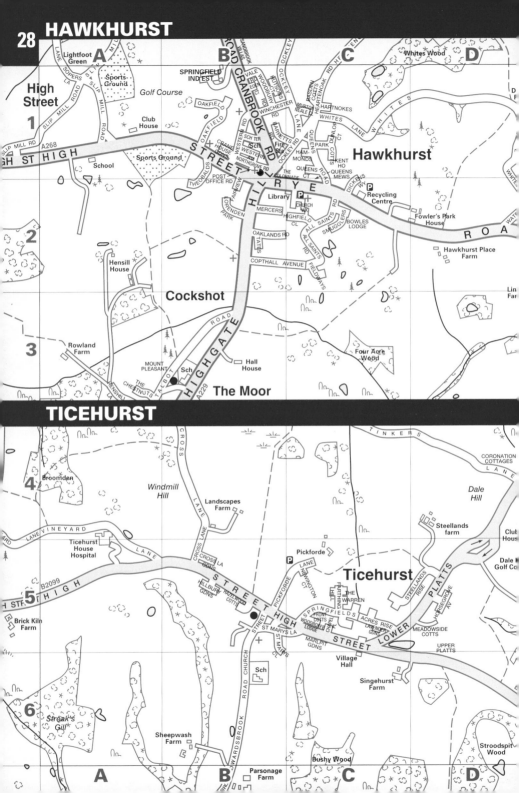

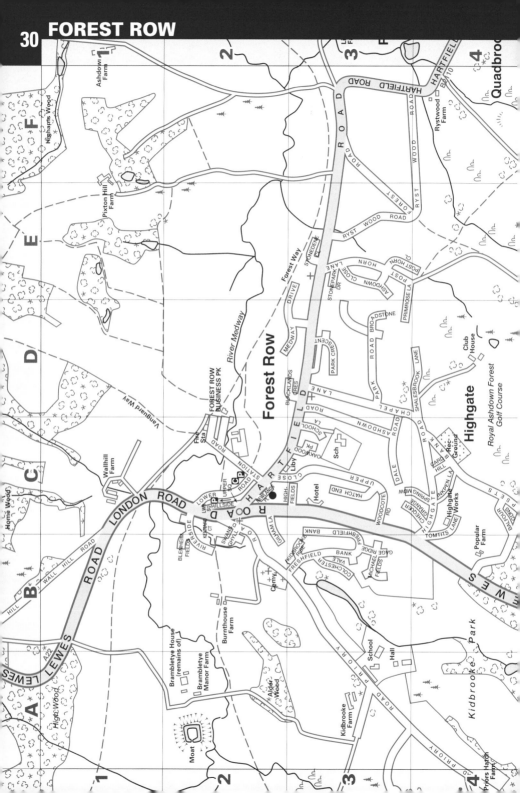

FOREST ROW

Highgate

Quadbrook

Royal Ashdown Forest Golf Course

A - Z INDEX TO STREETS
with Postcodes

Index includes some
nes for which there is
[su]fficient space on the
[ma]p. These names are indi-
[cat]ed by an * and are fol-
[low]ed by the nearest adjoin-
[ing] thoroughfare.

er Av TN2 17 F6
rn Cl TN12 24 C3
es Rise TN5 28 C5
... 22 C3
illestead Rd TN12 26 B2
any Cl TN9 9 G5
any Hill TN2 15 E6
ert Rd TN9 9 E4
ert St TN1 3 D1
ion Rd TN1 15 E6
ion Way TN8 29 B2
er Cl TN4 15 F2
erbrook Cl TN6 22 B3
erbrook Cotts TN6 22 B3
erbrook Path TN6 22 B3
erbrook Way TN6 22 B3
ers Cotts TN12 24 A5
ers Mdw TN9 8 C2
ers Rd TN12 24 A4
ervale Cotts TN6 22 B2
wych TN10 6 A3
wych Cl TN10 6 A3
xandra Rd,
Mayfield TN20 23 D4
xandra Rd,
onbridge TN9 9 E4
xandra Ter TN20 23 D4
se Bright La TN6 22 A2
Saints Rd,
Cranbrook TN18 28 C2
Saints Rd,
unbridge Wells TN4 14 D5
Saints Rise TN4 14 D5
n Cl TN4 13 F5
andale Rd TN2 15 F5
ance Way TN12 25 F3
ngton Dr TN10 6 C5
ngton Rd TN12 25 F3
berleaze Dr TN2 18 D3
berley Cl TN9 8 D4
herst Rd TN4 14 C6
hurst Bank Rd TN2 24 A5
drew Rd TN4 15 E3
drews Cl TN2 15 F6
gel La TN9 9 E3
gel Walk TN9 9 E3
gley Ct TN12 26 B5
gley Rd TN17 27 A5
gley Walk TN17 27 C3
ole Ct TN12 25 F4
ole Tree La TN2 15 F3
oletons TN11 7 E3
oley St TN4 13 F5
ayle Rd TN4 14 D1
ne Cl TN10 6 B4
undel Cl TN9 8 D4
undel Rd TN1 3 D5
n Cl,
Edenbridge TN8 29 B5
n Cl,
unbridge Wells TN2 17 F6
burnham Rd TN10 9 F1
bys Cl TN8 29 C6
bys Yd TN9 9 F3
ncombe Dr TN8 29 B2
ncroft Rd TN12 25 G5
nden Walk TN10 5 H3
ndown Cl,
Forest Row RH18 30 E3
ndown Cl,
unbridge Wells TN4 16 B1
ndown Ct TN6 20 C4
ndown Rd RH18 30 C3
nenden Walk TN12 15 G3
ner Reeds TN3 13 D5
nes La TN11 6 B1
nlands TN6 21 F5
nleigh Gdns TN6 20 C2
nley Gdns,
Mayfield TN20 23 B5
nley Gdns,
unbridge Wells TN4 13 E5
nley Park Rd TN4 13 E5
nley Pk TN4 13 E5
nley Rd TN11 4 D5

Aspen Way TN4 15 F2
Auckland Rd TN1 15 E5
Audley Av TN9 8 C3
Audley Rise TN9 8 C3
Aultmore Ct TN2 17 F2
Avebury Av TN9 9 E3
Avenue Le Puy TN9 9 F4
Aviemore Rd TN4 20 B4
Avon Cl TN10 5 H5
Avon St TN1 15 E6

Back La TN12 26 B4
Badgers Cl TN6 20 C3
Badgers Holt TN2 15 G6
Badsell Rd TN12 24 C3
Bakers Cross TN17 27 C5
Bakers Ter TN17 27 C5
Balaclava La TN5 19 E1
Baldock Rd TN5 19 D3
Balfour Gdns RH18 30 D4
Ballard Way TN12 25 H3
Balliol Cotts TN5 19 F4
Baltic Rd TN9 9 E5
Bank St,
Cranbrook TN17 27 B4
Bank St, Tonbridge TN9 9 E2
Bankside TN5 19 D2
Banner Farm Rd TN2 3 D6
Barchester Way TN10 6 C4
Barclay Av TN10 6 C6
Barden Park Rd TN9 8 D3
Barden Rd,
Tonbridge TN9 8 D3
Barden Rd,
Tunbridge Wells TN3 10 A5
Bardsley Cl TN12 26 C1
Barham Dr TN17 27 C4
Barn Hawe TN8 29 C5
Barnetts Cl TN4 15 E3
Barnetts Rd TN11 10 B2
Barnetts Way TN4 15 E3
Barnfield,
Crowborough TN6 21 E4
Barnfield,
Tonbridge TN12 26 C1
Barons Cl TN4 14 D6
Barretts Rd TN18 28 B1
Barrow La TN3 13 C7
Basden Cotts TN18 28 C1
Bassetts Forge TN5 19 D3
Batchelors Cl TN2 18 E2
Bayhall Rd TN2 17 E2
Bayham Cl TN5 19 D2
Bayham Rd TN2 16 C5
Beacon Cl TN6 20 C4
Beacon Gdns TN6 20 C3
Beacon Rd TN6 20 A6
Beacon Rd West TN6 20 B4
Beagles Wood Rd TN2 18 E2
Beaulieu Rd TN10 5 G6
Beaumont Ct TN2 16 C4
Beaver Cl TN6 21 E5
Bedford Rd TN4 14 C2
Bedford Ter TN1 3 B5
Beech Hurst TN2 18 D3
Beech Manor TN2 17 F3
Beech St TN1 3 D1
Beecham Rd TN6 6 B4
Beeches Farm Rd TN6 21 E5
Beeches Rd TN6 21 E5
Beechmont Rise TN10 5 G4
Belfield Rd TN2 18 D4
Belgrave Rd TN1 3 C1
Belgrove TN1 3 C5
Beltring Rd TN4 14 C5
Belvedere Gdns TN6 21 E6
Benhall Mill Rd TN2,3 17 E5
Bentham Hill TN3 14 A2
Bentley Path TN6 22 E2
Berkeley Cl TN2 18 E3
Berkeley Pl*,
Berkeley Rd TN1 3 C5
Berkeley Rd TN1 3 B6
Beulah Rd TN1 17 E1
Beverley Cres TN4 8 C5
Bickley Rd TN9 9 F3
Bickmore Way TN9 9 F1
Bidborough Ridge
TN3,4 11 E4
Birch Cl,
Tunbridge TN11 4 D6

Birch Cl,
Tunbridge Wells TN2 15 F5
Birch Rd TN12 25 G4
Birch Way TN2 15 F4
Birchden Cotts TN3 23 D3
Birchden Rd TN3 23 D3
Birches Cl TN6 20 D2
Birchetts Av TN3 13 B6
Birchwood Av TN4 11 F5
Bird La TN5 19 A3
Birdcage Walk TN1 3 C5
Birken Rd TN2 15 F5
Birling Dr TN2 16 D5
Birling Park Av TN2 16 D5
Birling Rd TN2 16 D5
Bishops Ct TN4 16 B2
Bishops Down Park Rd
TN4 16 B1
Bishops Down Rd
TN4 16 B2
Bishops Oak Ride
TN10 5 G4
Blackberry Way TN12 25 H4
Blackhurst La TN3 15 H6
Blacklands Cres RH18 30 D3
Blackmans La TN11 7 C3
Blackness Rd TN6 20 D5
Blacksmiths La TN5 19 F2
Blackthorn Av TN4 15 E3
Blake Ct*,
Brook Rd TN2 15 F4
Blakeway TN2 15 F4
Blatchington Rd TN2 16 D4
Blenheim Flds RH18 30 B2
Bliss Way TN10 6 B5
Bocking La TN5 19 D3
Bondfield Cl TN4 14 D2
Booker Cl TN6 21 E5
Bordyke TN9 9 F2
Botany TN9 9 F3
Boundary Rd TN2 17 F4
Bounds Oak Way TN4 11 F4
Bourne Cl TN9 9 G1
Bourne Grange La
TN11 7 C3
Bourne La TN9 9 F1
Bowen Rd TN4 13 E5
Bowles Lodge TN18 28 C2
Bowls Pl TN12 25 G3
Boyle Way TN12 26 D3
Boyne Pk TN4 3 A2
Boyne Pk TN4 16 C1
Bracken Cl,
Crowborough TN6 21 G5
Bracken Cl,
Tunbridge Wells TN2 15 G6
Bracken Rd TN2 15 G6
Bracken Walk TN10 5 G4
Bradford St TN9 9 E3
Bramble Cft TN6 21 E4
Bramble Cl TN11 5 E6
Bramble Walk TN4 15 F4
Bramley Dr TN17 27 C5
Bramley Gdns TN2 25 F3
Bramley Rd TN12 26 B2
Branbridges Rd TN12 26 D1
Brantingham Cl TN9 8 C5
Breedon Av TN4 14 C2
Brenchley Rd TN12 26 A5
Brendon Cl TN2 15 F6
Bretland Rd TN4 13 F5
Brewers Wood TN20 23 B5
Brian Cres TN4 14 D3
Briar Cl TN8 29 C3
Briar Walk TN10 5 H4
Brick Kiln La TN12 26 D6
Brickenden Rd TN17 27 C5
Brickfields TN2 18 E2
Brickmead TN6 21 E5
Brickworks Cl TN4 15 D6
Bridge Cl TN9 9 F4
Bridge Cotts TN12 26 B4
Bridge Ct TN4 16 B4
Bridger Way TN6 20 D5
Bright Ridge TN4 14 B3
Brincliffe TN6 20 C3
Brindles Fld TN9 8 D5
Brionne Gdns TN9 9 G4
Britten Cl TN10 6 B4
Broad Gro TN2 16 C5
Broad Oak TN3 23 C2
Broad Oak Cl TN2 16 C5

Broadcloth TN17 27 C6
Broadcroft TN2 16 C5
Broadmead TN2 16 B5
Broadmead Av TN2 16 B5
Broadstone RH18 30 D3
Broadwater Down
TN2 16 A5
Broadwater La TN2 16 B4
Broadwater Rise TN2 16 C4
Broadway,
Crowborough TN6 20 D3
Broadway*, High St,
Tonbridge TN11 7 D3
Brokes Way TN4 15 E3
Brook Cl TN6 21 G5
Brook Ct TN8 29 C3
Brook La TN9 9 G2
Brook Rd TN2 15 F4
Brook St TN9 8 C4
Brook Ter TN6 20 B2
Brook Vw TN6 20 B2
Brookfield Ct TN4 14 C2
Brookfields TN11 7 D2
Brookhurst Gdns TN4 11 F5
Brooklands TN2 15 F5
Brooklands Av TN6 22 B2
Brookmead TN11 4 D5
Brooks Cl TN10 6 A3
Brookside TN17 27 C5
Broom La TN3 13 B6
Broom Pk TN3 13 B7
Broomhill Park Rd
TN4 14 B3
Broomhill Rd TN3 12 F4
Broomwaters TN11 7 C1
Brownings TN8 29 B2
Brungers Walk TN10 5 G6
Brunswick Ter TN1 3 B6
Bryants Flds TN6 20 C3
Buckingham Rd TN1 3 C5
Bucklers Cl TN2 17 E2
Bullen La TN12 26 A1
Buller Cl TN6 21 E5
Bullfinch Cl TN12 25 G5
Bullingstone Cotts
TN3 12 B2
Bullingstone La TN3 12 B2
Bullion Cl TN12 25 F4
Bulls Pl TN2 18 D3
Burdett Rd,
Crowborough TN6 21 G5
Burdett Rd,
Tunbridge Wells TN4 13 E5
Burns Cres TN9 8 D5
Burnt House La TN3 12 C4
Burnt Oak Rd TN6 22 B4
Burrswood Villas TN3 23 C1
Burslem Rd TN2 16 C5
Bush Rd TN12 26 B1
Bushy Gill TN3 13 C6
Buttercup Cl TN12 25 G3
Byng Rd TN4 16 B3
Byrneside TN11 4 D6

Cabbage Stalk La
TN4 16 A4
Cadogan Gdns TN1 3 C3
Cage Green Rd TN10 5 H5
Caistor Rd TN9 8 D3
Caley Rd TN2 15 F4
Calverley Ct TN1 17 E2
Calverley Gdns TN1 3 D3
Calverley Park Cres
TN1 3 D3
Calverley Park Gdns
TN1 3 D3
Calverley Pk TN1 3 D3
Calverley Pk TN1 3 C2
Calverley St TN1 3 D2
Cambrian Rd TN4 15 E4
Cambridge Gdns TN2 3 D5
Cambridge St TN2 17 E2
Camden Av TN2 18 C4
Camden Ct,
Pembury TN2 18 D4
Camden Ct,
Tunbridge Wells TN1 3 D1
Camden Hill TN2 3 D5
Camden Pk TN2 17 E3
Camden Rd TN1 3 C2
Campbell Rd TN4 14 C5
Cannon La TN9 9 G2
Canterbury Cres TN10 6 A5

Canterbury Rd TN2 18 E4
Card Hill RH18 30 C4
Cardinal Cl TN9 9 G5
Carlton Cl TN10 6 A3
Carlton Cres TN1 17 E2
Carlton Rd TN1 17 E2
Carpenters La TN11 7 C1
Carriers Rd TN17 27 C4
Carville Av TN4 14 C2
Castle Flds TN9 9 E2
Castle Rd TN4 3 A3
Castle St,
Southborough TN4 14 C1
Castle St,
Tonbridge TN9 9 E2
Castle St,
Tunbridge Wells TN1 3 B5
Castle Ter TN11 7 D3
Castle Walk TN5 19 D3
Catherine Pl TN1 3 D3
Causton Ct TN17 27 B4
Cavalry Cl TN10 6 A3
Cavendish Cl TN10 6 A3
Cavendish Ct TN9 9 G2
Cavendish Dr TN2 3 D6
Caxton La TN11 7 D3
Caysers Cft TN12 26 A3
Cedar Cres TN10 5 H3
Cedar Ct TN4 14 C6
Cedar Dr TN8 29 B4
Cedar Lodge TN4 16 B2
Cedar Ridge TN2 15 F6
Cemetery Ct TN6 22 B1
Cemetery La TN11 7 E2
Chaffinch Way TN12 25 G5
Chalket La TN2 18 C4
Challenger Cl TN12 25 F4
Chancellor Ho TN4 16 B2
Chandos Rd TN1 15 E6
Chantlers Hill TN12 25 G6
Chapel La RH18 30 D3
Chapel Pl,
Tunbridge Wells TN1 3 B6
Chapel Pl,
Wadhurst TN5 28 C5
Chapman Way TN9 15 E3
Charity Farm Way TN6 21 E3
Charles Cl TN2 17 F2
Charles St TN4 14 C3
Charlottes Cotts TN11 10 A2
Charlton Ter TN9 9 F2
Charltons Way TN4 16 A4
Chaucer Gdns TN9 8 C5
Chenies Cl TN2 16 C6
Chequer Grange
RH18 30 C4
Chequers Cl TN6 21 E4
Chequers Way TN6 21 E4
Cherry Gardens Hill
TN3 23 A3
Cherry Gro TN10 6 B5
Cherry Tree Rd TN2 16 B4
Cherwell Cl TN10 5 G6
Chesfield Cl TN11 7 E2
Chester Av TN2 17 F3
Chestnut Av TN4 14 D3
Chestnut Cl,
Edenbridge TN8 29 B4
Chestnut Cl,
Tunbridge Wells TN4 14 D3
Chestnut Walk TN9 8 C2
Cheviot Cl TN9 5 H6
Chichester Rd TN9 8 D4
Chidley Cross Rd
TN12 26 B2
Chieveley Dr TN2 17 F5
Chilston Cl TN4 14 D6
Chilston Rd TN4 14 D6
Chiltern Walk TN2 17 F1
Chiltern Way TN9 9 F1
Chilternhurst TN8 29 A3
Christchurch Av TN1 3 C5
Church Cotts TN17 27 B4
Church Fld TN8 29 C5
Church Hill TN11 10 B2
Church La,
East Peckham TN12 26 B1
Church La,
Five Oak Green
TN12 24 A4
Church La,
Tonbridge TN9 9 F2
Church Rd,

Crowborough TN6 20 C4
Church Rd,
Hildenborough TN11 4 C4
Church Rd,
Paddock Wood TN12 25 G3
Church Rd,
Southborough TN4 14 B1
Church Rd,
Tunbridge Wells TN1 3 A3
Church St,
Edenbridge TN8 29 C5
Church St, Hadlow TN11 7 D3
Church St,
Ticehurst TN5 28 B6
Church St,
Tonbridge TN9 9 F2
Church St,
Wadhurst TN5 19 F3
Church Walk TN18 28 C2
Civic Way TN11 3 C3
Clackhams La TN6 22 F2
Clanricarde Gdns TN1 3 B3
Clanricarde Rd TN1 3 B3
Clare Av TN9 8 C3
Claremont Gdns TN2 3 D6
Claremont Rd TN1 3 C5
Clarence Rd TN1 3 B3
Clarence Row TN1 3 B3
Clarendon Gdns TN2 16 C4
Clarendon Way TN2 16 C5
Clavadal Rd TN12 25 G3
Cleeve Av TN2 17 G3
Cleveland TN2 17 F1
Clifford Ct TN6 20 C4
Clifton Cotts TN2 15 F3
Clifton Pl TN1 3 C6
Clifton Rd TN2 15 F4
Clockhouse TN2 18 A3
Clover Walk TN8 29 C3
Clover Way TN12 25 G4
Clyde Rd TN10 5 G4
Coach Rd TN4 13 F5
Cobbets Way TN8 29 B6
Cobbetts Ride TN2 16 B4
Cobbs Cl TN12 25 F4
Cobhams TN3 12 D2
Cockmount La TN5 19 E2
Cogate Rd TN12 25 F4
Coggins Mill La TN20 23 D4
Colchester Vale RH18 30 B3
Coldharbour Cl TN6 20 D5
Coldharbour Cotts TN6 22 B2
Coldharbour La TN11 4 D4
Colebrook Rd TN4 15 E4
Coles Ct TN2 17 E2
Colin Blythe Rd TN10 6 B5
College Av TN9 8 D5
College Dr TN2 17 F1
Colne Rd TN10 5 G5
Colonels Way TN4 14 D1
Colts Hill Pl TN12 24 C5
Combe End TN6 20 D6
Commerce Way TN8 29 B3
Commercial Rd,
Paddock Wood TN12 25 F4
Commercial Rd,
Tonbridge TN9 9 F4
Commercial Rd,
Tunbridge Wells TN1 16 D1
Common Rd TN11 7 D1
Common Vw TN4 13 E6
Common Wood Rise TN6 20 D2
Concord Cl,
Paddock Wood TN12 25 F3
Concord Cl,
Tunbridge Wells TN2 17 F1
Coneyburrow Rd TN2 15 G6
Coniston Av TN4 14 B6
Connaught Way TN4 14 B6
Constable Rd TN10 6 B5
Constitution Hill Rd TN4 14 B2
Coomb Fld TN8 29 B5
Coopers La TN6 20 B2
Coopers Wood TN6 20 B2
Copper Beech Vw TN9 8 D4
Copse Rd TN11 4 D6
Copthall Av TN18 28 B2
Cornfield Way TN10 6 A4
Cornford Cl,
Crowborough TN6 21 E5
Cornford Cl,
Pembury TN2 18 C3
Cornford La,
Pembury TN2 18 B4

Cornford La,
Tunbridge Wells TN2 17 G1
Cornford Pk TN2 18 C4
Cornwallis Av TN10 6 B6
Coronation Cotts TN5 28 D4
Correnden Rd TN10 8 D1
Corseley Rd TN3 23 C1
Cotman Way TN12 26 B2
Court La TN11 7 E3
Court Lane Pl TN11 7 E3
Court Rd TN4 16 B1
Courtenwell TN3 13 B5
Courthope TN12 25 G4
Courthope Av TN5 19 E3
Courtlands TN10 8 D1
Courtlands Pl TN6 20 C5
Cousley Wood Rd TN5 19 E2
Coventry Rd TN10 5 H5
Cranbrook Rd TN18 28 B1
Crandalls TN11 10 B2
Crane House Gdns TN18 28 B1
Crane La TN17 27 C5
Cranford Rd TN10 6 C5
Cranwell Rd TN4 13 F5
Crates Yd TN4 14 C6
Crendon Pk TN4 14 C3
Crescent Rd TN1 3 C3
Crittenden Rd TN12 24 C6
Crittles Ct TN5 19 E3
Crockford Cl TN10 6 A3
Croft Cl TN10 6 C6
Croft Cl TN8 29 C5
Croft La TN8 29 C5
Croft Rd TN6 20 D4
Croham Rd TN6 20 D3
Cromer St TN9 8 D3
Cromwell Rd TN2 17 E2
Cross La TN5 28 D5
Cross Lane Gdns TN5 28 B5
Crouch House Cotts TN8 29 A4
Crouch House Rd TN8 29 A2
Crowborough Hill TN6 20 D3
Crown Acres TN12 26 C2
Crown Ct TN17 27 B4
Crown Rd TN8 29 D2
Crundwell Rd TN4 14 B2
Cuckoo La TN11 6 C3
Culverden Av TN4 14 C5
Culverden Ct*,
Culverden Sq TN4 16 D1
Culverden Down TN4 14 B6
Culverden Park Rd TN4 14 C6
Culverden Pk TN4 14 C6
Culverden Sq TN4 3 B1
Culverden St TN1 8 D1
Cumberland Cl TN10 8 D1
Cumberland Gdns TN1 3 B6
Cumberland Mews TN1 3 B6
Cumberland Walk TN1 3 B6
Cumberland Yd TN1 3 B6
Cunningham Cl TN4 14 D4
Cunningham Rd TN4 14 D4
Currie Rd TN4 14 D6
Cypress Gro TN2 17 F5

Dairy Grn TN6 22 E2
Dale Rd RH18 30 C3
Dale St TN1 3 D1
Danvers Rd TN9 9 E3
Darenth Av TN10 5 G5
Darnley Dr TN4 11 E4
Darwin Dr TN10 6 A4
Deacon Ct TN4 14 C6
Deakin Leas TN9 9 E5
Deans Ct*,
Priory Gro TN9 9 E4
Deepdene TN5 19 F1
Delarue Cl TN11 6 A2
Delius Dr TN10 6 B4
Delves Av TN2 17 E4
Denbeigh Dr TN10 5 H4
Denbigh Rd TN4 15 E4
Dene Way TN3 12 C3
Denington Ct TN4 11 G5
Derby Cl TN11 4 D4
Dernier Rd TN10 5 H6
Derwent Dr TN4 14 B6
Derwent Rd TN10 5 G5
Devonshire Cl TN2 16 B5
Dickens Way TN18 28 C2
Dillon Way TN2 15 F5

Dimmock Cl TN12 25 H3
Dobwells TN17 27 C5
Doctor Hopes Rd TN17 27 C5
Dodd Rd TN10 6 B5
Dodshill TN6 21 E5
Doggets Cl TN8 29 B6
Donkey Fld TN11 10 A2
Doon Brae TN4 14 C1
Doric Av TN4 14 B2
Doric Cl TN4 14 B2
Dorin Ct TN1 17 E1
Dorking Rd TN1 15 E5
Dornden Dr TN3 13 C5
Dorothy Av TN17 27 C6
Dorset Rd TN2 17 F3
Douglas Rd TN9 8 D4
Dove Rd TN10 5 G6
Dowding Way TN2 15 G2
Dower House Cres TN4 11 F4
Dowgate Cl TN9 9 G5
Drage Rd TN12 26 B2
Draper St TN4 14 C1
Dray Ct TN11 7 D3
Drayton Rd TN9 9 F5
Driffield Gdns TN9 8 C5
Dry Bank Ct TN10 9 F1
Dry Bank Rd TN10 9 F1
Dry Hill Park Cres TN10 9 F1
Dry Hill Park Rd TN10 9 E1
Dry Hill Rd TN9 9 E1
Dudley Lodge*,
Ferndale Ct TN1 17 E1
Dudley Rd TN1 3 B2
Dukes Rd TN1 17 E1
Dunlop Ct TN18 28 C1
Dunorlan Ct TN2 17 F1
Dunstan Gro TN4 14 D6
Dunstan Rd TN4 14 D5
Dunstan Ter TN5 19 E2
Dunstans Cft TN20 23 D4
Dynevor Rd TN4 15 E4

Earls Rd TN4 16 B1
East Beeches Rd TN6 21 E4
East Cliff Rd TN4 14 C5
East St,
Mayfield TN20 23 D4
East St, Tonbridge TN9 9 F2
Eastfield Gdns TN10 6 B5
Eastlands Cl TN4 16 A5
Eastlands Est TN4 25 F2
Eastlands Rd TN4 16 A5
Eastwell Cl TN12 25 F3
Eden Ct TN18 28 B1
Eden Ct TN1 3 B6
Edward St,
Rusthall TN4 13 E5
Edward St,
Southborough TN4 14 C2
Eldon Way TN12 25 F2
Elgar Cl TN10 6 B4
Elim Court Gdns TN6 20 C2
Elizabeth Garlick Ct TN1 3 D1
Ellison Cl TN6 20 C2
Elm Cotts TN8 29 B2
Elm Gro TN11 5 E6
Elm La TN10 9 F1
Elm Rd TN4 14 C2
Elmhurst Av TN2 18 D1
Elmhurst Gdns TN10 5 H3
Elphick Pl TN6 20 D3
Elphicks Pl TN2 16 D5
Ely Ct TN1 3 C2
Ely Gdns TN10 6 A3
Ensfield Rd TN11 10 A3
Enterprise Way TN8 29 B3
Eridge Ct*,
Broadwater La TN2 16 B4
Eridge Dr TN6 21 E3
Eridge Gdns TN6 21 E3
Eridge Rd,
Crowborough TN6 20 D3
Eridge Rd,
Groombridge TN3 23 D3
Eridge Rd,
Tunbridge Wells TN3,4 3 A6
Erskine Park Rd TN4 13 E5
Essex Cl TN12 16 B5
Estridge Way TN10 6 C5
Etherington Hill TN3 12 E2
Ewehurst La TN3 12 B3
Ewins Cl TN10 25 G4
Exeter Cl TN10 5 H6

Fairacre TN3 13 C6

Faircrouch La TN5 19 A1
Fairfield Av TN5 15 F6
Fairfield Cres TN9 9 F5
Fairfield Way TN11 4 D5
Fairglen Cotts TN5 19 A4
Fairglen Rd TN5 19 A4
Fairlight Cl TN4 14 D1
Fairlight Ct TN10 5 G6
Fairmead Rd TN8 29 B1
Fairmile Rd TN2 15 G6
Fairview TN18 28 B2
Fairview Ct TN9 9 E6
Fairview Cotts TN6 20 C2
Fairview La TN6 20 C2
Falmouth Pl TN12 24 C3
Faraday Ride TN10 6 A3
Farm La TN6 5 F6
Farmcombe Cl TN2 3 D6
Farmcombe La TN2 3 C5
Farmcombe Rd TN2 3 D6
Farmground TN9 9 G4
Farmstead Dr TN8 29 C3
Farnham Beeches TN3 13 C5
Farnham Cl TN3 13 C6
Farnham La TN3 13 C6
Farnham Pl TN3 13 C6
Farningham Rd TN6 21 G6
Farthing Hill TN5 28 C5
Fazan Ct TN5 19 E4
Fell Mead TN12 26 B2
Fellowes Way TN11 4 D5
Ferbies TN3 12 C2
Ferbies Cl TN3 12 C2
Ferdinand Ter TN3 23 C1
Fermor Rd TN4 22 B2
Fermor Row TN6 20 D6
Fermor Way TN6 20 D6
Ferndale TN2 15 F6
Ferndale Cl TN2 17 E1
Ferndale Gdns TN2 17 E1
Fernholt TN10 5 H3
Fernhurst Cres TN4 14 C1
Field Dr TN8 29 C3
Fielden La TN6 20 B6
Fielden Rd TN6 20 B3
Fieldways TN18 28 C2
Figg La TN6 20 D6
Fir Toll Cl TN20 23 A5
Fir Toll Rd TN20 23 A5
Fir Tree Cl TN11 4 D5
Fir Tree Rd TN4 16 B3
Fircroft Way TN8 29 B3
First St TN3 13 B6
Five Oak Green Rd,
Five Oak Green TN12 24 A3
Five Oak Green Rd,
Tonbridge TN11 9 H5
Flaxmore Pl TN4 14 D1
Fleming Way TN10 6 A3
Fletching St TN20 23 C5
Florance La TN3 23 B2
Florence Cotts*,
Croft Ct TN5 29 C5
Floyd Cl TN4 14 C4
Foalhurst Cl TN10 6 B6
Forest Ct TN2 17 F3
Forest Dene,
Crowborough TN6 21 G5
Forest Dene,
Tunbridge Wells TN2 17 E4
Forest Gro TN10 5 H5
Forest Lodge TN6 20 B6
Forest Pk TN6 20 B6
Forest Rd,
Forest Row RH18 30 E3
Forest Rd,
Tonbridge TN12 25 G4
Forest Rd,
Tunbridge Wells TN2 16 C6
Forest Rise TN6 21 G5
Forest Way,
Pembury TN2 18 D2
Forest Way,
Tunbridge Wells TN2 17 F4
Forge Cl TN8 29 C5
Forge Cl TN12 24 C2
Forge Rd TN4 14 C3
Forge Sq TN11 10 B2
Forge Way TN12 25 G3
Forstall TN3 13 D5
Fosse Bank Cl TN9 8 D5
Fosse Rd TN9 9 E2
Four Elms Rd TN8 29 C4
Foxbush TN11 4 B4
Foxglove Cl TN8 29 C5
Framley Rd TN10 6 C5
Francis Rd TN11 4 C4

Frank Woolley Rd TN10 6
Frankfield Rise TN2 16
Franks Hollow Rd TN3 10
Frant Fld TN8 29
Frant Rd TN2,3 3
Freight La TN18 27
Fremlin Cl TN4 13
Freshfield Bank RH18 30
Friars Way TN2 18
Friezland Rd TN4 15
Frog La TN1 3
Fromandez Dr TN12 26
Frome Ct TN10 5
Front Cotts TN5 28
Frythe Cl TN17 27
Frythe Cres TN17 27
Frythe Walk TN17 27
Frythe Way TN17 27
Fuggles Cl TN12 2
Fuller Ct TN5 19
Furnace La TN12 25
Furnival Ct TN2 16
Furzefield Av TN3 12

Gage Ridge RH18 30
Gainsborough Gdns TN10 6
Garden Cotts TN11 10
Garden Rd,
Tonbridge TN9 9
Garden Rd,
Tunbridge Wells TN1 3
Garden St TN1 3
Gardyne Mews TN9 9
Garlands TN11 4
Garlinge Rd TN4 14
Garrick Cl TN10 6
Gate Farm Rd TN3 10
Gate House Fm TN3 10
George St,
Tonbridge TN9 9
George St,
Tunbridge Wells TN2 17
George St,
Wadhurst TN5 19
Ghyll Rd TN6 20
Gibbet La TN12 26
Gibbetts TN3 13
Gilham La RH18 30
Gillridge Grn TN6 20
Gimble Way TN2 18
Gipps Cross La TN3 13
Gladstone Rd,
Crowborough TN6 20
Gladstone Rd,
Tonbridge TN9 9
Gladstone Rd,
Tunbridge Wells TN4 13
Glebelands TN3 10
Glendale Ct TN2 15
Glenmore Pk TN2 16
Glenmore Rd TN6 20
Glenmore Rd East TN6 20
Gloucester Rd TN5 19
Goddards Cl TN17 27
Godfrey Evans Cl TN10 6
Goldfinch Cl TN12 25
Golding Gdns TN12 26
Goldings TN12 25
Goldsmid Rd TN9 9
Goldsmith Av TN6 20
Golford Rd TN17 27
Goods Station Rd TN1 3
Gordon Henry Ho TN8 29
Gordon Rd,
Crowborough TN6 20
Gordon Rd,
Tunbridge Wells TN4 15
Gorham Dr TN9 9
Gorse Rd TN12 15
Goudhurst Rd,
Cranbrook TN17 27
Goudhurst Rd,
Tonbridge TN12 26
Grainger Walk TN10 6
Grampion Cl TN2 15
Granary TN12 25
Grange Cl,
Crowborough TN6 20
Grange Cl,
Edenbridge TN8 29
Grange Gdns TN4 13
Grange Rd TN4 13
Grantley Cl TN1 3
Granville Rd TN1 15
Graycoats Dr TN6 20

at Bounds Dr TN4 11 F4
at Brooms Rd TN4 15 E3
at Courtlands TN3 13 C5
at Elms TN1 7 D2
at Footway TN3 13 C6
at Hall Arc TN1 3 C4
at Mead TN8 29 B3
cian Rd TN1 3 C5
en La,
  rowborough TN6 21 F4
en La,
  onbridge TN12 25 G5
en Rd TN12 26 B5
en Sq TN5 19 E3
en View Av TN11 10 B2
en Way TN12 15 G3
enfield TN8 29 C4
enfield Cl TN4 12 E4
enfrith Dr TN10 5 G3
enleas TN2 18 C3
entrees Av TN10 6 B5
enview Cres TN11 4 D6
enway TN17 27 A5
ggs Wood Rd TN2 15 G4
sham Cl TN10 6 A3
shams Way TN8 29 A4
menfield TN3 23 C2
ombridge Hill TN3 23 C1
svenor Bri TN1 15 E6
svenor Pk TN1 3 B1
svenor Rd TN1 3 B1
svenor Walk TN1 3 C1
ve Av TN1 3 C5
ve Hill Gdns TN1 3 D5
ve Hill Rd TN1 3 C4
vehurst La TN12 26 D6
ver St TN1 3 D2
rds Cl TN10 6 A3
stwick TN10 6 C5
dford Rd TN1 3 C5
La TN12 26 B5
alands TN12 26 B4
lley Ct TN4 14 C5
low Down Rd
  N6 22 C4
low Pk TN11 7 E2
low Rd TN10 6 C6
low Rd TN9 6 C6
low Stair Rd TN10 6 C6
stone Cl TN11 7 D3
e Ct TN12 26 D1
e St TN12 26 D1
e Moon La TN11 4 C4
and Ct TN8 29 B5
s Cotts TN5 19 E2
s Hole Rd TN2 17 F3
nble Rd TN10 5 G5
nilton Ct TN4 14 D6
nilton Ho*,
  lamilton Ct TN4 14 D6
nmonds TN18 28 C1
del Walk TN10 6 B5
over Rd TN1 3 B2
dinge Av TN4 11 E5
dwick Rd TN1 4 D4
ecombe Rd TN6 20 C6
ecombe Rise TN6 20 D6
escroft TN2 16 C6
gate Cl TN2 16 B6
land Way TN4 11 F4
lequin La TN6 20 C5
lequin Pl TN6 20 C6
mer Ct TN4 14 C2
mony St TN4 16 A1
ries Rd TN2 15 F4
row Cl TN8 29 C3
tfield Cl TN10 6 B5
tfield Rd RH18 30 C2
tley Rd TN17 27 A6
tnokes TN18 28 C1
vest Rd TN10 5 H4
letts Cl TN1 15 E6
tings Rd TN2 18 D4
ch End RH18 30 C3
ches La TN12 26 A2
velock Rd TN9 9 E2
vering Cl TN2 15 H5
vden Cl TN11 5 E6
vden La TN11 8 C1
vden Rd TN9 9 E2
vkenbury Cl TN2 17 F4
vkenbury Mead
  N2 17 F4
vkenbury Rd TN2 17 F4
vthorn Cl TN8 29 B4
vthorn Walk,
  onbridge TN10 5 H3
vthorn Walk,

Tunbridge Wells TN2 15 G3
Haydens Mews TN9 9 F1
Hayesden La TN11 10 B4
Haymans Hill TN12 26 D4
Haywain Cl TN12 25 G5
Hazel Shaw TN10 5 H4
Hazelbank TN3 13 C6
Hazelwood Cl TN2 15 G3
Hazelwood Cotts TN5 28 B5
Headley Cl TN8 29 C4
Headway Ct TN4 13 E5
Heartenoak Rd TN18 28 C1
Heather Bank TN12 25 H4
Heather Walk,
  Crowborough TN6 21 G5
Heather Walk,
  Tonbridge TN10 5 G3
Heathfields TN2 17 F1
Heathview TN4 14 B1
Heavegate Rd TN6 20 A5
Hectorage Rd TN9 9 F4
Helen Keller Ct TN10 5 H6
Hendley Dr TN17 27 B4
Henham Gdns TN12 26 C2
Henley Cl TN2 17 F1
Henley Rd TN12 25 G3
Henshill La TN18 28 A3
Henwood Green Rd
  TN2 18 E2
Henwoods Cres TN2 18 E4
Henwoods Mount
  TN2 18 E4
Herne Down TN6 22 B2
Herne Rd TN6 20 D6
Heron Cl TN8 29 C3
Herons Way TN2 18 E2
Heskett Pk TN2 18 E3
Hever Rd TN8 29 C6
High Beeches TN2 15 F5
High Broom La TN6 22 A3
High Broom Rd TN6 22 A2
High Brooms Rd TN4 15 E3
High Cross Flds TN6 20 D3
High Hilden Cl TN10 5 F6
High House La TN11 6 D2
High Rocks La TN3 13 E8
High St,
  Bidborough TN3 10 D4
High St,
  Cranbrook TN17 27 A5
High St,
  Crowborough TN6 20 D3
High St,
  Edenbridge TN8 29 C5
High St, Hadlow TN11 7 D3
High St,
  Hawkhurst TN18 28 A1
High St, Leigh TN11 10 A1
High St, Mayfield TN20 23 B5
High St, Pembury TN2 18 A5
High St, Ticehurst TN5 28 A5
High St, Tonbridge TN9 9 E4
High St,
  Tunbridge Wells TN1 3 B5
High St,
  Wadhurst TN5 19 E3
High Woods La TN2 17 F3
Higham Gdns TN10 6 C5
Higham La TN11 6 B1
Higham School Rd
  TN10 6 B4
Highfield Cl,
  Cranbrook TN17 28 B2
Highfield Cl,
  Tunbridge Wells
  TN2 18 D3
Highfield Rd TN14 15 E4
Highfields RH18 30 C2
Highfields Rd TN8 29 B1
Highgate Hill TN18 28 B3
Highgate Rd RH18 30 C4
Highgrove TN2 16 D5
Highlands Cl TN6 20 C3
Highlands Ho*,
  Calverley Rd TN2 17 E2
Hilbert Cl TN2 15 E6
Hilbert Rd TN2 15 E5
Hilden Av TN11 5 E6
Hilden Park Rd TN11 5 E6
Hildenborough Rd
  TN11 10 B1
Hilders Cl TN8 29 B1
Hilders Farm Cl TN8 21 F5
Hilders Farm Ct TN6 21 F5
Hilders La TN8 29 A2
Hill Cl TN6 20 C5
Hill St TN1 3 C1
Hill Top TN9 9 E5

Hill View Rd,
  Tonbridge TN11 5 E5
Hill View Rd,
  Tunbridge Wells TN14 13 E5
Hillbury Gdns TN5 20 B3
Hillcrest Dr TN2 15 F4
Hillcrest Rd TN8 29 B1
Hillgarth TN4 14 D4
Hillrise TN6 21 F4
Hillside,
  Forest Row RH18 30 C2
Hillside, Tonbridge TN9 8 D5
Hither Chantlers TN3 13 D6
Hoadleys La TN6 20 D1
Hoath Mdw TN12 26 B4
Hobbs Ct TN10 6 C5
Holden Corner TN4 14 B2
Holden Park Rd TN4 14 C3
Holden Rd TN4 14 B2
Holford St TN9 9 E3
Hollin Cl TN4 16 B1
Hollow Trees Dr TN11 10 C2
Holly Cotts TN8 29 A4
Holly Ct TN6 20 A4
Hollydene Rd TN5 19 E1
Hollyshaw Cl TN2 17 E3
Holmewood Rd TN4 15 E4
Holmewood Ridge
  TN3 13 B6
Holmhurst Cl TN4 16 B2
Holmsdale Cl TN5 19 D2
Home Farm La TN2 15 G3
Homestead Rd TN8 29 B1
Homewood Rd TN3 13 B6
Hookswood Cl TN6 21 E3
Hop Pocket La TN12 25 G2
Hope Av TN11 7 C2
Hope Ter TN4 14 C6
Hopgarden Cl TN8 29 C3
Hopgarden Rd TN10 6 A5
Hopwood Gdns TN4 14 D5
Horizon Cl TN4 16 B3
Hornbeam Av TN4 15 F2
Hornbeam Cl TN12 25 F5
Horns Lodge La TN11 10 A1
Horsegrove Av TN5 28 D5
Houselands Rd TN9 9 E2
Howard Gdns TN2 16 C4
Humboldt Ct TN6 15 F6
Hungersall Park Cl
  TN4 16 A4
Hungershall Pk TN4 16 A4
Hunt Rd TN10 6 B4
Hunters Way TN2 16 B4
Huntingdon Cl TN17 27 C5
Huntingdon Rd TN6 20 D6
Huntleys Pk TN4 14 B6
Hurlingham La TN10 6 A3
Hurstwood La TN4 16 B2
Hurstwood Pk TN4 16 B2
Hurtis Hill TN6 22 A2
Hutsons Cl TN18 28 B1
Hydehurst Cl TN6 20 D5
Hythe Cl TN4 14 C2
Imber Ct TN17 27 C5
Impala Gdns TN4 14 D5

INDUSTRIAL & RETAIL:

Angel Centre TN9 9 F3
Arnold Bsns Pk TN12 26 D3
Botany Ind Est TN9 9 F3
Branbridges Ind Est
  TN12 26 D3
Bridge Bsns Pk TN12 24 C2
Cannon Bridge Works
  TN9 9 G2
Colebrook Ind Est
  TN2 15 G2
Deacon Trading Est
  TN9 9 G3
Durgates Ind Est TN5 19 D2
Edenbridge Trading
  Centre TN8 29 C6
Eldon Way Ind Est
  TN12 25 F2
Fernbank Centre TN6 20 C3
Forest Row Bsns Pk
  RH18 30 D2
Goblands Farm Ind Est
  TN11 7 F3
Goods Station Rd Trading
  Est TN1 3 C1
Guardian Bsns Pk
  TN2 15 H1
King Standing Bsns Pk
  TN2 15 H2
Knights Pk Leisure
  Complex TN2 15 H3

Lexden Lodge Ind Est
  TN6 21 G6
Millbrook Bsns Pk
  TN6 21 H6
Millbrook Ind Est
  TN6 21 H6
Munday Works Est
  TN9 9 F3
North Farm Ind Est
  TN2 15 F3
Orchard Bsns Centre,
  Tonbridge TN9 9 H3
Orchard Bsns Centre,
  Tunbridge Wells TN2 15 F3
Paddock Wood Distribution
  Centre TN12 25 H2
Riverdale Ind Est TN9 9 G4
Royal Tunbridge Wells
  Bsns Pk TN2 15 G2
Royal Victoria Pl Shopping
  Centre TN1 3 C2
Spa Ind Pk TN2 15 G3
Springfield Ind Est
  TN18 28 B1
Transfesa TN12 25 G2
Valley Industries TN11 6 D3
Wadhurst Bsns Pk
  TN5 19 A1
Warsop Ind Est TN8 29 D6
Wealdon Ind Est TN6 22 D2

Ingleside Dr TN6 20 C4
Inhams Wood TN6 20 B2
Inkpen La RH18 30 C4
Inner London Rd TN1 3 B3
Ironstones TN3 13 E6
Ives Rd TN9 8 C3
James Cl TN11 7 E2
Jardine Ct TN6 20 D4
Jasmine Cotts TN2 23 C1
Jeffries Way TN6 20 D2
Jempsons TN17 27 B4
Jockey La TN4 27 C4
John Spare Ct*,
  Whitefield Rd TN4 14 C6
John St TN4 14 C6
Jonas Dr TN5 19 D2
Jonas La TN5 19 D2
Joyce Cl TN17 27 B5
Judd Rd TN9 9 E5
Juniper Ct TN4 15 F2
Kates Ct TN9 9 E2
Katherine Rd TN8 29 C6
Katherine Villas*,
  Katherine Rd TN8 29 C6
Keel Gdns TN8 14 B3
Kelvin Cl TN10 6 A3
Kemble Ct TN2 15 G4
Kemps Farm Rd TN6 21 F5
Kendal Cl TN9 9 F2
Kendal Dr TN9 9 F2
Kendal Pk TN4 14 A6
Kennard Ct RH18 30 B2
Kennet Rd TN10 5 G5
Kent Cl TN12 25 G3
Kent Ho TN18 28 C1
Kent Rd TN4 14 C5
Kentish Gdns TN2 16 B6
Kenward Ct TN11 7 D3
Kestrel Cl TN8 29 C3
Keswick Cl TN9 9 F2
Keyes Gdns TN9 8 C5
Keyworth Cl TN12 25 F3
Kibbles La TN4 14 B2
Kidbrooke Rise RH18 30 B3
Kiln La TN11 10 A2
Kiln Way TN12 25 G5
King George V Hill TN2 15 E6
King Standing Way
  TN2 15 H1
Kings Chase TN6 20 B3
Kings Ct,
  Crowborough TN6 20 C4
Kings Ct,
  Tonbridge TN12 26 B4
Kings Pk TN2 17 F2
Kings Rd TN9 9 F5
Kings Toll Rd TN2 18 F3
Kingsley Ct TN5 19 F3
Kingswood Ct TN2 17 E2
Kingswood Rd TN2 17 E2
Kinnings Row TN9 9 F2
Kirby Cl TN17 27 C5
Kirby Ct TN3 13 D6
Kirkdale Rd TN1 3 D1
Kirkins Cl TN12 26 B4
Knight Rd TN10 6 A4

Knights Cl TN2 18 D2
Knights Pk TN2 15 H3
Knights Ridge TN2 18 D3
Knights Way TN2 15 H3
Knightsbridge Cl TN14 14 B6
Knowle Cl,
  Crowborough TN6 22 B2
Knowle Cl,
  Tunbridge Wells
  TN3 13 B6
Knowle Hill TN20 23 A6
Knowle Pk TN6 20 B4
Knowle Rd TN20 23 A6
Knowsley Way TN11 4 C4
Laburnum Ct*,
  Sandhurst Rd TN2 15 F4
Ladyfern Ct*,
  Ferndale TN2 17 F1
Ladys Gift Rd TN4 14 B3
Lake Rd TN4 16 B1
Lakeside TN2 15 G5
Lamberhurst Rd TN12 26 A6
Lambersart Cl TN4 15 F3
Lamberts Pl TN12 26 C5
Lamberts Rd TN2 15 F3
Lambourn Way TN2 17 F4
Lambs Bank TN9 9 E6
Lampington Row TN3 13 A6
Landseer Cl TN10 6 A4
Langholm Rd TN3 13 A3
Langton Rd,
  Langton Green TN3 13 A7
Langton Rd,
  Speldhurst TN3 12 C4
Langton Ridge TN3 13 D6
Langton Ter TN3 13 D6
Lansdowne Rd,
  Tonbridge TN9 9 E2
Lansdowne Rd,
  Tunbridge Wells TN1 3 D3
Lansdowne Sq TN1 3 D2
Larch Cres TN10 5 H4
Larch Gro TN12 25 G4
Larkfield TN12 24 B3
Laurel Bank,
  Tunbridge Wells TN4 14 C6
Laurel Bank,
  Wadhurst TN5 19 F4
Laurel Rd TN2 15 F4
Laurel Way TN2 15 F4
Lavender Gdns TN5 28 C5
Lavender Hill TN9 9 F5
Lawn Rd TN9 9 F4
Lawrence Rd TN10 6 B4
Laxton Gdns TN12 25 F3
Le Temple Rd TN12 25 H3
Lealands Av TN11 10 B2
Lealands Cl TN3 23 C2
Leather Cl TN8 29 B6
Leathermarket TN8 29 C5
Leconfield Cl TN9 8 C5
Leggs La TN3 12 A4
Leicester Dr TN2 16 B5
Leigh Rd TN11 4 C6
Leighton Cl TN4 14 C4
Leneda Dr TN2 16 B5
Leslie Tew Ct TN10 5 G5
Lewes Cl RH18 30 A1
Lewes Rd RH18 30 B4
Leybank TN11 5 E6
Lime Hill Rd TN1 3 B2
Lime Tree Cl TN9 9 F2
Limekiln Ct TN6 21 F3
Lincoln Way TN6 22 B2
Linden Cl,
  Tonbridge TN12 25 G4
Linden Cl,
  Tunbridge Wells TN4 3 A6
Linden Ct TN10 5 G3
Linden Gdns TN2 16 C4
Linden Park Rd TN4 3 A6
Lingfield Rd TN8 29 A6
Link Way TN2 15 G4
Links Cl TN6 20 B5
Linnet Av TN12 25 G5
Lionel Rd TN9 8 D4
Lipscombe Rd TN2 15 F5
Liptraps La TN2 15 F4
Little Bounds TN4 11 F4
Little Footway TN3 13 C6
Little Mallett TN3 13 B6
Little Mount Sion TN1 3 B5
Little Paddocks TN6 20 C5
Little Pk TN5 19 D3
Little Sunnyside TN6 20 D5
Loampits Cl TN9 9 G1
Lockington Cl TN9 8 C5
Lockside TN9 9 F2

33

Lodge Oak Rd TN9 9 G5
Lodge Rd TN9 9 E2
Lomaria Ct*,
  Ferndale Cl TN1 17 E1
London Rd,
  Crowborough TN6 20 B1
London Rd,
  Forest Row RH18 30 C1
London Rd,
  Hildenborough TN11 4 A2
London Rd,
  Southborough TN4 11 F4
London Rd,
  Tonbridge TN11 5 E6
London Rd,
  Tunbridge Wells TN1 3 A3
Lonewood Way TN11 7 E1
Long Mead Way TN10 5 G6
Long Meads TN3 13 D6
Long Slip TN3 13 D6
Longfield Rd TN2 15 F3
Longview Way TN2 15 F4
Lonsdale Gdns TN1 3 A5
Lordswell La TN6 20 C6
Lorenden Pk TN18 28 B2
Love La TN20 23 A5
Lovers Walk TN9 9 F1
Lower Green Rd,
  Pembury TN2 18 D4
Lower Green Rd,
  Tunbridge Wells TN3 12 E2
Lower Grn TN11 10 A2
Lower Haysden La
  TN11 8 A5
Lower High St TN5 19 F3
Lower Platts TN5 28 C5
Lower Rd RH18 30 C2
Lower Saxonbury TN6 20 D4
Lower Sq RH18 30 C2
Lower St TN11 14 A5
Loxfield Cl TN20 23 A5
Loxfield Gdns TN6 21 F5
Lucilina Dr TN8 29 B6
Lucknow Rd TN12 25 G2
Lucks La TN12 25 G1
Luxford Dr TN6 21 E6
Luxford La TN6 21 E6
Luxford Rd TN6 22 C2
Lynmead Cl TN8 29 B2
Lynwood TN3 23 C2
Lyons Cres TN9 9 F3
Lyons Wharf TN9 9 F3

Mableden Rd TN9 8 D4
Macdonald Ct TN12 25 G4
Madeira Pk TN2 3 C6
Magnolia Cl TN9 9 F5
Magpie Grn TN8 29 C3
Maidstone Rd,
  Colts Hill TN12 24 B6
Maidstone Rd,
  Hadlow TN11 7 E3
Maidstone Rd,
  Horsmonden TN12 26 B4
Maidstone Rd,
  Paddock Wood TN12 25 F4
Maidstone Rd,
  Tunbridge Wells TN2 18 E2
Main Rd TN8 29 B1
Major Yorks Rd TN4 3 A6
Mallard Way TN8 29 C3
Maltings Cl TN11 7 D3
Malton Way TN2 15 H5
Mann Sq TN9 9 G5
Manor Cl TN4 16 B2
Manor Gro TN10 9 F1
Manor House Gdns
  TN8 29 B5
Manor Pk TN4 16 B2
Manor Rd,
  Edenbridge TN8 29 B5
Manor Rd,
  Rusthall TN4 13 E5
Manor Rd,
  Southborough TN4 14 B2
Manor Way TN6 20 C6
Maple Cl TN2 16 C4
Mardens Hill TN6 20 A1
Market Pl TN2 3 A6
Market Sq TN1 3 D2
Market St TN2 3 A6
Marlborough Cl TN4 16 B1
Marlhurst TN8 29 B2
Marlpit Cl TN8 29 C2
Marlpit Gdns TN5 28 C5
Marshall Gdns TN11 7 D2
Martin Hardie Way TN10 6 A5
Marvillion Ct TN12 26 C2

Mary Magdalene Ho
  TN9 9 E4
Maryland Rd TN2 17 F4
Mascalls Court La
  TN12 25 H6
Mascalls Court Rd
  TN12 25 G5
Mascalls Pk TN12 25 F5
Masefield Way TN9 8 C5
Mayfield Cl TN20 23 A5
Mayfield La TN5 19 A4
Mayfield Pk TN5 19 C3
Mayfield Rd TN4 16 B1
Maylam Ct TN10 5 G6
Maynards Mead TN5 28 D5
Meadow Bank TN11 10 B2
Meadow Hill Rd TN1 3 C5
Meadow La TN8 29 B2
Meadow Rd,
  Groombridge TN3 23 C2
Meadow Rd,
  Rusthall TN4 13 E5
Meadow Rd,
  Southborough TN4 14 C2
Meadow Rd,
  Tonbridge TN9 9 E4
Meadow Rd,
  Tunbridge Wells TN1 3 C1
Meadowside Cotts
  TN5 28 D5
Meadway TN11 4 D5
Medina Rd TN10 5 G4
Medway TN6 21 F4
Medway Dr RH18 30 D2
Medway Mdws TN12 26 D2
Medway Rd TN1 15 E6
Medway Wharf Rd
  TN9 9 F3
Melfort Rd TN6 20 B5
Mendip Walk TN2 17 F1
Mercer St TN1 16 D1
Mercers,
  Cranbrook TN18 28 B2
Mercers,
  Tunbridge Wells TN3 13 C6
Mercers Cl TN12 25 F4
Mereworth Rd TN4 14 C5
Merlin Cl TN10 6 B6
Merrion Cl TN4 15 E4
Merrion Way TN4 15 E4
Merryfield Ct*,
  Quarry Gdns TN9 9 E4
Mersey Rd TN10 5 G5
Michael Flds RH18 30 B3
Middle Fld TN2 18 E2
Middle Garth TN17 27 C5
Middle Walk TN2 15 G4
Middlefield TN4 13 E5
Mill Cres,
  Crowborough TN6 20 D3
Mill Cres,
  Tonbridge TN9 9 F2
Mill Dr TN6 20 D3
Mill Hill TN8 29 C6
Mill Hill Cotts TN8 29 C6
Mill La,
  Crowborough TN6 20 C4
Mill La,
  Hildenborough TN11 4 A3
Mill La, Tonbridge TN9 9 F2
Mill Stream Pl TN9 9 G1
Mill Vw TN11 7 C2
Millbrook Rd TN6 20 D4
Milton Dr TN2 15 F4
Milton Gdns TN9 8 C5
Mitre Ct TN9 9 F2
Moat Farm TN2 16 C6
Modesty Cotts TN4 14 A2
Moles Mead TN8 29 B4
Molescroft Way TN9 8 C5
Molyneux Cl TN4 16 B1
Molyneux Park Gdns
  TN4 3 A2
Molyneux Park Rd TN4 3 A2
Monks Walk*,
  Priory Walk TN9 9 E4
Monson Colonade*,
  Monson Rd TN1 3 C2
Monson Rd TN1 3 C2
Monson Way TN1 3 C3
Mont St Aignan Way
  TN8 29 C5
Montacute Gdns TN4 3 A6
Montacute Rd TN2 16 C4
Montargis Way TN6 20 D5
Monteith Cl TN3 13 D6
Montgomery Rd TN4 14 D4
Monypenny Cl TN11 7 C2
Morley Dr TN12 26 B4

Morley Rd TN9 9 G3
Mottins Hill TN6 22 F2
Mount Edgecombe Rd
  TN4 3 A4
Mount Ephraim TN1 3 A3
Mount Ephraim Ct TN4 3 A3
Mount Ephraim Rd
  TN1 3 B2
Mount Pleasant,
  Cranbrook TN18 28 A3
Mount Pleasant,
  Crowborough TN6 22 D2
Mount Pleasant,
  Hildenborough TN11 4 C4
Mount Pleasant,
  Tonbridge TN12 25 F3
Mount Pleasant,
  Tunbridge Wells TN5 19 D2
Mount Pleasant Av TN1 3 C3
Mount Pleasant Ct TN11 14 C4
Mount Pleasant Rd
  TN1 3 C4
Mount Sion TN1 3 B5
Mountfield Ct TN1 3 C4
Mountfield Gdns TN1 3 C4
Mountfield Pk TN9 9 F5
Mountfield Rd TN1 3 C4
Mulberry Cl TN4 15 F2
Murton Neale Cl TN18 28 C1
Myrtle Rd TN6 20 D5

Napier Rd TN2 17 F3
Nellington Rd TN4 12 D4
Nelson Av TN9 8 D3
Nelson Rd TN2 17 F3
Nevill Cl TN6 20 A6
Nevill Ct TN6 20 A6
Nevill Gate TN2 16 D4
Nevill Lodge*,
  Ferndale Cl TN1 17 E1
Nevill Pk TN4 16 A2
Nevill Rd TN6 20 D3
Nevill Ridge TN4 13 F6
Nevill St TN2 3 B6
Nevill Ter TN4 16 C4
New Bassetts Cotts
  TN12 26 C5
New Ct TN9 9 F2
New Dr TN3 23 B3
New England Rd TN4 14 D5
New Rd,
  Cranbrook TN17 27 A5
New Rd,
  Crowborough TN6 20 D3
New Rd,
  Tonbridge TN12 25 G4
New Wharf Rd TN9 9 E3
Newbarn Ct TN10 5 H4
Newcombe Wood
  TN2 16 D5
Newcomen Rd TN4 14 C6
Newhouse Ter TN8 29 B3
Newick La TN20 23 B6
Newington Ct TN5 18 C5
Newlands TN3 13 D6
Newlands Pl RH18 30 C2
Newlands Rd TN4 14 D5
Newlands Rise TN4 14 D5
Newlands Way TN4 14 D4
Newton Av TN10 6 A3
Newton Gdns TN12 25 F3
Newton Rd TN1 3 C2
Newton Willows TN3 23 D2
Noble Tree Rd TN11 4 A4
Norbury Cl TN6 20 C2
Norfolk Cl,
  Tonbridge TN9 8 D3
Norfolk Rd,
  Tunbridge Wells TN1 3 C5
Norman Rd TN1 3 D1
Norman Rise TN17 27 C6
Norstead Gdns TN4 14 D4
North Beeches Rd
  TN6 21 E5
North Farm Rd TN2 16 D5
North Frith Pk TN11 6 B1
North St,
  Mayfield TN20 23 B4
North St,
  Tunbridge Wells TN2 17 E2
North Trench TN10 5 G4
Northcote Rd TN9 9 E4
Northdown Cl TN12 25 F3
Northfield TN3 12 C2
Northgrove Rd TN18 28 B1
Northwood Rd TN10 5 G4
Norton Cres TN10 5 G3
Norton Rd TN4 14 C2
Nortons Way TN12 24 B3

Norwich Av TN10 6 A6
Nottidge Rd TN4 16 A5
Nursery Cl TN10 6 A6
Nursery Rd,
  Tonbridge TN12 25 F2
Nursery Rd,
  Tunbridge Wells TN4 15 E3
Nye Cl TN6 20 D5

Oak End Cl TN4 14 C1
Oak Rd,
  Tonbridge TN12 24 B3
Oak Rd,
  Tunbridge Wells TN2 15 F4
Oak Ter*,
  Cranbrook Rd TN18 28 B1
Oak Tree Cl TN2 16 D4
Oak Vw TN8 29 B4
Oakdale Rd TN4 16 B1
Oakfield TN18 28 B1
Oakfield Ct TN2 17 E3
Oakfield Ct Rd TN2 17 E3
Oakfield Rd TN8 29 B1
Oakhurst Dr TN6 21 E3
Oakland Villas TN3 23 C2
Oaklands TN6 21 E5
Oaklands Rd,
  Cranbrook TN18 28 B2
Oaklands Rd,
  Tunbridge Wells TN3 23 C2
Oaklands Way TN11 5 E6
Oaklea Rd TN12 25 G4
Oakmead TN10 5 H4
Oakwood Pk RH18 30 C3
Oakwood Rise TN12 15 G3
Oast Cl TN2 15 F4
Oast La TN10 5 F6
Oast Vw TN12 26 B5
Oatfield Cl TN17 27 A4
Oatfield Dr TN17 27 A4
Ockley La TN18 28 B1
Ockley Rd,
  Cranbrook TN18 28 B1
Ocklye Rd,
  Crowborough TN6 20 A4
Old Barn Cl TN9 8 D4
Old Cannon Wharf
  TN9 9 G3
Old Church Rd TN2 18 D1
Old Gardens Cl TN2 16 D5
Old Hadlow Rd TN10 6 B6
Old Kent Rd TN12 25 G4
Old La,
  Crowborough TN6 21 F5
Old La, Mayfield TN20 23 A5
Old La, St Johns TN6 20 B3
Old London Rd TN10 9 F1
Old Mill Ct TN6 26 C2
Old Rd TN12 26 C2
Old Station Rd TN5 19 D1
Oliver Cl TN4 21 E5
Orchard Cl,
  Edenbridge TN8 29 A4
Orchard Cl,
  Tonbridge TN12 26 A4
Orchard Cl,
  Tunbridge Wells TN2 15 F5
Orchard Cres TN12 26 B4
Orchard Dr,
  Edenbridge TN8 29 A4
Orchard Dr,
  Tonbridge TN10 6 B5
Orchard Lea TN11 5 E5
Orchard Rd TN12 26 C2
Orchard Rise TN3 23 B2
Orchard Way,
  Cranbrook TN17 27 A6
Orchard Way,
  Tonbridge TN12 26 B4
Orchidhurst TN2 15 F4
Osborne Hill TN6 21 G6
Osborne Rd TN6 21 G6
Osmers Hill TN5 19 E1
Osmunda Ct*,
  Ferndale Cl TN1 17 E1
Ospringe Pl TN2 15 H4
Ox Lea TN3 13 D6
Oxfield TN8 29 C3

Palesgate La TN6 21 F2
Palmers Brook TN11 7 E1
Park Av,
  Edenbridge TN8 29 B4
Park Av,
  Tonbridge TN11 5 E5
Park Cl TN11 7 D2
Park Cotts TN18 28 C1
Park Ct TN4 16 C1
Park Cres,
  Crowborough TN6 2
Park Cres,
  Forest Row RH18 3
Park House Gdns TN4 1
Park La TN6 2
Park Rd,
  Crowborough TN6 2
Park Rd,
  Forest Row RH18 3
Park Rd,
  Southborough TN4 1
Park Rd,
  Tunbridge Wells TN41
Park St TN2 1
Park View Cl TN8 2
Park Villas TN11
Parklands TN4 1
Parkway TN10 1
Parkwood Cl TN2 1
Parsonage Cl TN4 1
Parsonage Rd TN4 1
Pattenden Gdns TN12 2
Peach Hall TN10
Pear Tree Cl TN17 2
Peckham Ct TN12 2
Pell Cl TN5 1
Pell Hill TN5 1
Pellings Farm Cl TN6 2
Pemble Cl TN12 2
Pembroke Rd TN9
Pembury Cl TN2 18
Pembury Grange TN2 18
Pembury Gro TN9
Pembury Rd,
  Pembury TN11 18
Pembury Rd,
  Tonbridge TN9 9
Pembury Rd,
  Tunbridge Wells TN21
Pen Way TN10
Pendrill Pl TN5 19
Penfolds Cl TN10
Penlee Cl TN8
Pennine Walk TN2 1
Pennington Pl TN4 14
Pennington Rd TN4 14
Pennyfields TN17 27
Penshurst Rd,
  Leigh TN11 10
Penshurst Rd,
  Penshurst TN3,11 10
Penshurst Rd,
  Speldhurst TN3,11 12
Percy Ter TN4 14
Petersfield TN2 1
Philpots La TN11 4
Piccadilly La TN20 23
Pickforde La TN5 28
Pilmer Rd TN6 20
Pine Gro TN6 2
Pine Gro TN8 29
Pine Ridge TN10 5
Pinewood Chase TN6 20
Pinewood Cl TN12 25
Pinewood Ct TN4 25
Pinewood Gdns TN4 1
Pinewood Rd TN12 15
Pink Alley TN2 3
Pinkham TN12 2
Pinkham Gdns TN12 2
Pipers Cl TN5 19
Pippin Rd TN12 2
Pit La TN8 29
Pittswood Cotts TN11 6
Plane Walk TN10 5
Pleasant View Rd TN6 20
Plough Walk TN2 29
Plover Cl TN8 2
Polesden Rd TN2 17
Polley Cl TN2 18
Pollington Pl TN6 20
Poona Rd TN1 3
Poppy Mdw TN12 25
Portland Cl TN10 6
Portman Pk TN9 9
Post Horn Cl RH18 30
Post Horn La RH18 30
Post Office Rd TN18 28
Postern La TN11 9
Pound Rd TN12 26
Poundfield Farm TN6 21
Poundfield Rd TN6 21
Poundsbridge Hill TN3 12
Powder Mill La TN4 14
Powder Mills TN11 14
Powdermill Cl TN4 15
Powdermill La TN12 14
Pratts Folly La TN6 20
Preston Rd TN9 8

stley Dr TN10 6 A3
mers Green Rd
N5 19 E2
rose La RH18 30 D3
rose Walk TN12 25 G5
ces St TN2 17 E2
ry Gro TN9 9 E4
ry Rd,
orest Row RH18 30 A4
ry Rd,
onbridge TN9 9 E4
ry St TN9 9 E4
ry Walk TN9 9 E4
spect Pk TN4 14 B2
spect Rd,
outhborough TN4 14 B2
spect Rd,
unbridge Wells TN2 3 D5
vidence Cotts TN3 23 C1
cell Av TN10 6 C5
enden Rd TN11 6 B1

ker Dr TN17 27 C3
ker La TN17 27 C3
ntock Cl TN2 17 F1
rry Bank TN9 8 D5
rry Cotts TN5 19 C1
rry Gdns TN9 9 E4
igh St TN9 9 E4
rry Hill Par*,
rry Hill Rd TN9 8 D6
rry Rd TN1 15 E6
rry Rise TN9 8 D5
ens Cotts TN5 19 D2
ens Ct,
ranbrook TN18 28 C1
ens Ct,
dens Gdns TN4 14 D5
ens Mews TN18 28 C1
ens Rd,
ranbrook TN18 28 C1
ens Rd,
rowborough TN6 20 D6
ens Rd,
unbridge Wells TN4 14 C6
ncewood Gdns
N10 5 G3

burn Cl TN10 6 B4
amell Mews TN17 27 C5
aslye Rd TN4 16 A5
kine Rd TN2 15 F4
noch Rd TN6 20 B4
noch Rd West TN6 20 B4
hael Ct TN11 4 D3
enswood Av TN2 15 F6
tory Dr TN3 10 D4
tory Flds TN17 27 C4
tory La TN17 27 C4
bridge La TN6 22 A3
ipoll Walk TN12 25 G5
wood Pk TN12 24 A4
ency Hall TN2 3 A6
ent Pl TN2 17 F2
ina Ct TN4 16 B2
abrandt Cl TN10 6 B4
nolds Cl TN10 6 A4
nolds La TN4 14 B5
ton Gdns TN12 25 F3
ardson Rd TN4 14 D6
mead Gdns TN20 23 B5
mond Pl TN2 16 D5
llesdale Av TN4 14 D5
ie Way TN8 29 C2
gelands TN3 10 D4
geway TN2 18 D2
geway Cres TN10 6 A6
ng La TN11 4 C1
ng Pk TN11 4 C3
gden Av TN12 25 F4
gs Hill TN11 4 A6
r Lawn Rd TN9 9 E3
r Mews TN8 29 D5
r Walk TN9 9 E3
rside,
denbridge TN8 29 C5
rside,
orest Row RH18 30 B2
rside Ct,
denbridge TN8 29 C5
rside Ct,
onbridge TN9 9 F3
rside Gdns TN6 29 C6
yns Way TN8 29 C6
hdale Rd TN1 15 E6
hester Ho TN6 21 G5
hester Rd TN10 6 A6

Rochester Way TN6 21 F5
Rochmans Way TN6 21 E6
Rock Villa Rd TN1 3 B2
Rockington Way TN6 21 F5
Rodmell Rd TN2 16 C4
Rodney Av TN10 6 B6
Rodwell Rd TN6 21 G5
Roedean Rd TN2 16 C4
Romford Rd TN2 18 E3
Romney Way TN6 6 A5
Rookley Cl TN2 17 F3
Roopers TN3 12 C2
Rope Walk TN17 27 B4
Ropers Gate TN4 16 B4
Rose St TN9 9 F4
Rosecroft Pk TN3 13 C5
Rosehill Gdns TN6 21 G5
Rosehill Walk TN1 3 B3
Roselands Av TN20 23 A6
Rossdale TN2 15 F6
Rother Cl TN6 22 B2
Rother Rd TN10 5 G5
Rotherfield La TN20 23 A4
Rotherfield Rd TN2 21 H6
Rotherhill Rd TN6 22 B2
Rothermead TN20 23 A6
Roundhill Rd TN2 17 F5
Rowan Cl TN12 25 F4
Rowan Shaw TN10 5 H4
Rowan Tree Rd TN2 16 B4
Rowfield TN8 29 C3
Royal Av TN9 9 F4
Royal Chase TN4 3 A1
Royal Oak Mews
TN20 23 B4
Royal Rise TN9 9 F4
Royal West Kent Av
TN10 5 H6
Ruffets Ct TN4 16 A4
Ruscombe Cl TN4 14 C1
Rushetts TN3 13 B5
Russells Yd TN17 27 C5
Russett Rd TN12 26 B2
Rusthall Grange TN4 13 F5
Rusthall High St TN4 13 E5
Rusthall Pk TN4 16 A2
Rusthall Rd TN4 13 F5
Rustwick TN4 16 A1
Rutherford Way TN10 6 A3
Rydal Cl TN4 14 A6
Rydal Dr TN4 14 A6
Ryders TN3 13 C6
Rye Rd TN18 28 B2
Rymers TN4 15 F4
Ryst Wood Rd RH18 30 E3

St Andrews Cl TN12 25 G3
St Andrews Cl TN4 14 C2
St Andrews Park Rd
TN4 14 C2
St Andrews Rd TN4 14 C2
St Barnabas Cl TN1 15 E6
St Bernards Rd TN10 5 H4
St Brelades Ct TN8 29 A3
St Davids Rd TN4 14 D5
St Denys Vw TN6 21 E5
St Dunstans Walk TN17 27 C5
St Georges Mews*,
George St TN9 9 E4
St Georges Pk TN2 16 C5
St James Cl TN10 6 A3
St James Ct TN1 3 D1
St James Pk TN1 15 E6
St James Rd TN1 15 E6
St Johns Cl TN6 20 C3
St Johns Pk TN4 14 C3
St Johns Rd,
Crowborough TN6 20 B2
St Johns Rd,
Tunbridge Wells TN4 14 C6
St Lawrence Av TN4 11 E4
St Lukes Rd TN4 14 D5
St Marks Rd TN2 16 B6
St Mary-in-the-Fields
TN20 23 B5
St Marys Cl TN5 28 B5
St Marys La,
Tunbridge Wells TN3 12 C2
St Marys La,
Wadhurst TN5 28 B5
St Marys Rd TN9 9 E5
St Michaels Cl TN6 21 F6
St Michaels Ct TN1 15 E6
St Michaels Rd TN4 14 D5
St Pauls Cl TN6 6 A5
St Pauls St TN4 13 E5
St Peters St TN2 17 E2
St Richards Rd TN6 22 C2
St Stephens Cotts*,

Stanley Rd TN4 14 D6
St Stephens St TN9 9 E4
St Thomas of Canterbury Ct
TN20 23 B5
Salisbury Cl TN10 6 A5
Salisbury Rd,
Langton Green TN3 13 B6
Salisbury Rd,
Tonbridge TN10 6 A6
Salisbury Rd,
Tunbridge Wells TN4 15 E3
Salomons Rd TN4 13 F5
Sanderson Way TN9 9 G3
Sandhurst Av TN2 18 E4
Sandhurst Cl TN2 15 F5
Sandhurst Pk TN2 15 F4
Sandhurst Rd TN2 15 H6
Sandown Cl TN2 15 H6
Sandown Gro TN2 15 H5
Sandown Pk TN2 15 H6
Sandridge TN6 20 C5
Sandrock Ho*,
Sandrock Rd TN2 17 F1
Sandrock Rd TN2 17 F1
Saunders Rd TN4 16 A5
Saville Cl TN10 6 A3
Saxby Wood TN11 10 A2
Saxonbury Cl TN6 20 D4
School Fld TN8 29 B4
School La,
Crowborough TN6 20 D5
School La,
Forest Row RH18 30 C3
School La,
St Johns TN6 20 B2
School La,
Tonbridge TN11 7 D3
School Rise TN2 16 B5
School Ter TN18 28 B1
Scott Rd TN9 8 C5
Scotts Way TN2 16 B5
Seabrook Rd TN10 8 D1
Sefton Chase TN6 21 E3
Sefton Way TN6 21 E3
Senlac Pl TN3 23 C1
Severn Cl TN10 5 H5
Shaftesbury Rd TN4 14 C6
Shakespeare Rd TN9 8 C5
Shalesbrook La RH18 30 D4
Shandon Cl TN2 17 E2
Shawfield TN6 21 F4
Sheafe Dr TN17 27 B4
Sheep Plain TN6 20 B5
Sheffield Rd TN4 14 C1
Sheiling Rd TN6 20 C3
Shelton Cl TN10 5 H5
Shepherds Walk,
Crowborough TN6 21 F5
Shepherds Walk,
Tunbridge Wells TN2 17 F2
Sherborne Cl TN2 17 G3
Sheridan Cl TN10 5 E6
Sherwood Rd TN2 15 F5
Sherwood Way TN2 15 G5
Shipbourne Rd
TN10,11 5 H6
Shirley Cotts*,
Woodbury Park Rd
TN4 14 D6
Shirley Gdns TN4 12 F4
Shirley Gro TN4 12 F4
Showfields Rd TN2 17 E1
Shrubland Cl TN2 17 E1
Shrublands TN9 9 F2
Sidney Cl TN2 16 B5
Silver Cl TN9 9 E6
Silverdale La TN4 15 E5
Silverdale Rd TN4 15 E5
Silverhurst Dr TN10 5 H4
Silwood Cl TN2 15 G5
Simons Cl TN6 21 E5
Sir Davids Pk TN4 14 B3
Siskin Cl TN12 25 G5
Siskin Gdns TN12 25 G5
Six Penny Cl TN8 29 C5
Skeynes Rd TN8 29 B5
Skinners La TN8 29 C3
Skinners Ter TN9 9 E4
Slip Mill Rd TN18 28 A1
Smithers Cl TN11 7 D2
Smithers Ct TN12 26 D1
Smithers La TN12 26 D1
Smithyfield TN8 29 D3
Smugglers TN18 28 C2
Smugglers La TN6 29 C6
Smythe Cl TN4 11 F5
Snape Vw TN5 19 H4
Snipe TN2 18 E2
Snoll Hatch Rd TN12 26 B3

Somerhill Rd TN9 9 G4
Somerset Rd TN4 14 C5
Somerset Villas TN3 23 C1
Somerville Gdns TN4 3 A2
Sopers La TN18 28 A1
Sorrell Cl TN8 29 C3
South Gro TN1 3 B5
South St,
Crowborough TN6 20 D5
South St,
Mayfield TN20 23 B5
South St,
Mayfield TN20 23 C5
South View Rd,
Tunbridge Wells TN4 15 E4
South View Rd,
Wadhurst TN5 19 E2
Southfield Rd TN4 14 C5
Southfields,
Tunbridge Wells TN3 12 C2
Southfields,
Wadhurst TN5 19 E1
Southfields Way TN4 14 D4
Southgate TN4 16 B2
Southmead Cl TN20 23 D4
Southridge Dr TN6 20 C6
Southridge Rise TN6 20 C6
Southview Rd TN6 20 B6
Southway Cl TN6 20 C5
Southwood Av TN4 14 D5
Southwood Rd TN4 12 E4
Sovereign Way TN9 9 F3
Spa Cl TN11 7 E2
Sparrows Grn Rd TN5 19 E3
Sparrows Grn*,
Sparrows Green Rd
TN5 19 E2
Speedwell Cl TN8 29 C3
Speldhurst Hill TN2 12 D2
Speldhurst Rd,
Langton Green TN3 12 B4
Speldhurst Rd,
Tunbridge Wells TN4 14 A3
Spelmonden Rd TN12 26 A6
Spencer Mews,
Berkeley Rd TN1 3 B5
Spencer Mews,
Camden Rd TN1 3 D2
Speyside TN10 5 G5
Spring Gdns TN4 13 E5
Spring La TN3 10 D5
Spring Mdw RH18 30 C4
Springfield Cl TN6 21 F4
Springfield Pl TN3 23 C1
Springfield Rd,
Edenbridge TN8 29 B5
Springfield Rd,
Groombridge TN3 23 C2
Springfield Rd,
Southborough TN4 14 C2
Springfields TN5 28 C5
Springhead TN2 15 F6
Springhead Way TN6 20 C6
Springwell Rd TN9 9 E5
Springwood Pk TN11 6 A2
Squirrel Way TN2 17 G1
Stabledene Way TN2 18 D4
Staces Cotts TN12 25 F5
Stacey Rd TN10 5 E6
Stackfield TN8 29 C3
Stafford Cl TN2 17 G1
Stafford Rd TN9 9 E2
Stag Rd TN2 15 G3
Stainer Rd TN6 6 B4
Stair Rd TN10 6 C6
Stanam Rd TN2 18 E4
Stanbridge Rd TN8 29 B4
Standen St TN4 14 C6
Stangrove Ct TN8 29 B4
Stangrove Rd TN8 29 B5
Stanhope Rd TN1 15 E6
Stanley Rd TN1 14 D6
Star La TN20 23 C5
Star Mews TN20 23 B5
Starfield TN6 20 C5
Station App,
Edenbridge TN8 29 C4
Station App,
Mayfield TN20 23 A5
Station App,
Tonbridge TN12 25 G3
Station Cotts TN12 26 C5
Station Rd,
Crowborough TN6 21 G6
Station Rd,
Edenbridge TN8 29 B4
Station Rd,
Forest Row RH18 30 C2
Station Rd,

Mayfield TN20 23 A5
Station Rd,
Tonbridge TN12 25 G3
Station Rd,
Tunbridge Wells TN3 23 C2
Station Rd,
Wadhurst TN5 19 A1
Steellands Rise TN5 28 C5
Steep Rd TN6 22 D3
Steers Pl TN11 7 D1
Stephens Rd TN4 14 D6
Stewart Rd TN4 15 E4
Still La TN4 14 C1
Stockenbury TN12 26 B3
Stockland Green Rd
TN3 12 E2
Stocks Green Rd TN11 4 A6
Stone Court La TN2 18 E2
Stone Cross TN20 23 A5
Stone Cross Rd,
Crowborough TN6 22 B3
Stone Cross Rd,
Wadhurst TN5 19 F4
Stone St,
Cranbrook TN17 27 C4
Stone St,
Tunbridge Wells TN5 3 D1
Stonebridge La TN5 19 D1
Stonecott Ct TN6 20 D6
Stonedene Cl RH18 30 E3
Stonepark Dr RH18 30 E3
Stonewall Park Rd TN3 13 B6
Stonewood Cl TN4 14 D3
Stoneyfield TN8 29 C3
Stour Cl TN10 5 G5
Stratford St TN1 15 E6
Strawberry Cl TN2 16 A6
Strawberry Vale TN9 9 F4
Stream Side TN10 6 A3
Streatfield TN8 29 C5
Strettitt Gdns TN12 26 C3
Stuart Cl TN2 16 B5
Sullivan Rd TN10 6 B5
Summerhill Av TN4 14 B2
Summervale Rd TN4 16 A4
Sunhill Ct TN2 18 C4
Sunnybank Cl TN20 23 C5
Sunnyside TN8 29 B2
Sunnyside Rd TN4 13 F5
Surrey Cl TN2 16 B5
Sussex Cl TN2 17 E4
Sussex Mews TN2 3 A6
Sussex Rd TN9 8 D4
Sutherland Rd TN1 3 C5
Swallow Dr TN2 15 H5
Swan La TN8 29 B2
Swan Ridge TN8 29 C2
Swanland Dr TN9 8 C5
Swanmead Way TN9 9 G2
Swans Ghyll RH18 30 B2
Swaylands Av TN6 22 B2
Sweeps Hill Cl TN2 18 D3
Swift Cl TN6 20 B5
Swifts Vw TN17 27 C3
Sybron Way TN6 21 H6
Sycamore Cotts TN2 18 C4
Sycamore Gdns TN12 25 G5
Sychem La TN12 24 B3
Sychem Pl TN12 24 A3

Tabor Ct*,
Maidstone Rd TN12 26 B4
Tainter Rd TN11 7 D2
Talbot Pk TN2 15 F6
Talbot Rd TN18 28 A3
Tamar Rd TN10 5 G5
Tanners Mead TN8 29 B5
Tanners Way TN6 21 E5
Tannery Rd TN9 9 F3
Tanyard Hill TN3 23 C3
Tapsells La TN5 19 B2
Tarbutts TN17 27 C5
Tarland Ho TN2 17 F3
Tates TN18 28 B2
Taylor Ct*,
Brook Rd TN4 15 F4
Taylor St TN4 14 D6
Tea Garden La TN3 13 E6
Tedder Rd TN4 14 D4
Teise Cl TN2 17 F3
Templars Ct TN8 29 C3
Thames Rd TN10 5 G5
The Avenue,
Mayfield TN20 23 C5
The Avenue,
Tonbridge TN9 9 E2
The Beeches TN2 9 E2
The Bines TN12 25 G5
The Birches TN9 9 E5

The Boundary TN3 13 E6
The Brent TN10 5 H4
The Cedars TN12 25 G3
The Chase,
Tonbridge TN10 5 G5
The Chase,
Tunbridge Wells TN2 3 D5
The Cherry Orch TN11 7 D2
The Chestnuts TN18 28 A3
The Close,
Crowborough TN6 20 C3
The Close,
Tunbridge Wells TN323 2 C2
The Colonnade TN18 28 B1
The Coppice TN2 18 D3
The Crescent,
Cranbrook TN17 27 C5
The Crescent,
Groombridge TN3 23 C1
The Crescent,
Southborough TN4 11 F4
The Crescent,
Tonbridge TN9 9 E2
The Crossway TN4 16 A3
The Drive,
Crowborough TN6 20 B4
The Drive,
Tonbridge TN9 9 E5
The Drive,
Tunbridge Wells TN216 D4
The Fairways TN4 14 D4
The Farthings TN6 21 E3
The Ferns TN1 17 E1
The Forstal,
Tonbridge TN11 7 E3
The Forstal,
Tunbridge Wells TN218 E2
The Forstall TN11 10 B2
The Freehold,
East Peckham TN12 26 C2
The Freehold,
Hadlow TN11 7 C2
The Gill TN2 18 E2
The Glade,
Mayfield TN20 23 B4
The Glade,
Tonbridge TN10 6 A3
The Glebe,
Bidborough TN3 10 D4
The Glebe,
Pembury TN2 18 D2
The Glebelands TN6 20 D4
The Glen TN4 11 H5
The Goodwins TN2 3 C1
The Green,
Crowborough TN6 20 D4
The Green,
Tonbridge TN11 10 B2
The Green,
Tunbridge Wells TN313 B6
The Green La TN11 10 B2
The Greenways TN12 25 F5
The Grove,
Crowborough TN6 20 C5
The Grove,
Mayfield TN20 23 B5
The Grove,
Tonbridge TN9 9 F2
The Grove,
Tunbridge Wells TN218 D1
The Haydens TN9 9 F1
The Hill TN17 27 C5
The Hollies TN20 23 B5
The Homestead TN3 23 C1
The Hoppers TN12 24 C2
The Hurst TN2 15 G4
The Leas TN5 19 F1
The Limes TN8 29 C5
The Lowry TN9 9 E4
The Maltings TN11 7 D3
The Manse TN20 23 B5
The Manwarings
TN12 26 B4
The Marlpit TN5 19 D2
The Martlets TN6 20 D5
The Meadow TN2 18 E2
The Meadows TN6 20 D4
The Meads TN2 17 F3
The Mews, Camden Rd,
Tunbridge Wells TN3 3 D1
The Mews, Grove Hill Rd,
Tunbridge Wells TN3 4 D4
The Mews,

Pembury TN2 18 C3
The Midway TN4 13 F6
The Nightingales*,
Queens Rd TN4 14 D6
The Paddock,
Tonbridge TN10 7 D2
The Paddock,
Tunbridge Wells TN218 C3
The Pantiles TN2 3 A6
The Park TN6 20 D4
The Pavilion TN9 9 E3
The Plat TN8 29 C5
The Ridge TN3 23 A2
The Ridgeway TN10 5 H5
The Ridgewaye TN14 D2
The Ridings,
Tonbridge TN12 25 G3
The Ridings,
Tunbridge Wells TN215 H5
The Shaw TN2 17 E4
The Shires TN2 25 G3
The Slade TN9 9 E2
The Spinney TN9 8 D5
The Square,
Edenbridge TN8 29 C5
The Square,
Hadlow TN11 7 D3
The Square,
Leigh TN11 10 B2
The Square,
Wadhurst TN5 19 F3
The Tanyard TN17 27 C5
The Twitten TN6 20 C5
The Violets TN12 25 G5
The Warren,
Mayfield TN20 23 D4
The Warren,
Wadhurst TN5 28 C5
The Woodlands TN2 17 F1
Theobalds TN18 28 B2
Theodore CI TN2 15 G4
Third St TN3 13 B6
Thirlmere Rd TN4 14 A6
Thomas St TN4 14 C6
Thornfield Gdns TN2 15 H6
Thorpe Av TN10 5 H5
Three Elm La TN11 6 D4
Three Oaks La TN5 19 B1
Tilebarn Corner TN10 6 A6
Tilsden La TN17 27 D5
Tinkers La TN5 28 C4
Tippens CI TN17 27 C5
Toby Gdns TN11 7 D3
Tolhurst Rd TN12 24 B3
Tollwood Pk TN6 21 F5
Tollwood Rd TN6 21 F5
Tompsets Bank RH18 30 C4
Tomtits La RH18 30 B4
Tonbridge By-Pass
TN11 4 A4
Tonbridge Chambers*,
Pembury TN2 9 E5
Tonbridge Rd,
East Peckham TN12 26 A4
Tonbridge Rd,
Hadlow TN11 7 A4
Tonbridge Rd,
Hildenborough TN11 4 B4
Tonbridge Rd,
Pembury TN2 18 A1
Torbay Rd TN12 26 D3
Town Acres TN10 5 H6
Town Mdw TN17 27 C5
Townlands Rd TN5 19 E3
Transfesa Rd TN12 25 G1
Trebilco CI TN2 15 F4
Treblers Rd TN6 22 F2
Tree Tops TN9 9 E6
Trench Rd TN10 5 G4
Trenches Rd TN6 20 D5
Trinity CI TN2 17 F2
Tristan Gdns TN4 13 F5
Troy CI TN6 21 E5
Truro Walk TN10 5 H5
Tubwell La TN6 22 E2
Tudeley La TN9 9 F5
Tudor Ct TN2 16 B5
Tulip Tree CI TN9 9 E4
Tunbridge Wells Rd
TN20 23 C4
Tunnel Rd TN1 3 C1
Turner Av TN17 27 C6
Turner Rd TN6 6 A5

Turners Green La TN5 19 E1
Turners Green Rd TN5 19 E1
Tutsham Way TN12 25 F3
Tuxford Rd TN4 12 E4
Tweed Rd TN10 5 H5
Twyford Rd TN11 7 D2
Twyfords TN6 20 C5
Tyne Rd TN10 5 G5

Union Sq TN4 3 A6
Upper CI RH18 30 C3
Upper Cumberland Walk
TN2 16 D4
Upper Dunstan Rd TN414 D5
Upper Grosvenor Rd
TN1 3 C1
Upper Hayesden La
TN11 8 A6
Upper Nellington TN3 13 D5
Upper Platts TN5 28 D5
Upper Profit TN3 13 C6
Upper Sq RH18 30 C2
Upper St TN4 16 A1
Upper Stephens TN3 13 D6
Upton Quarry TN3 13 B6
Uridge Cres TN10 5 H6
Uridge Rd TN10 9 F1

Vale Av,
Southborough TN4 14 C2
Vale Av,
Tunbridge Wells TN1 3 B4
Vale Ct TN4 14 C1
Vale Rd,
Cranbrook TN18 28 B1
Vale Rd,
Mayfield TN20 23 C5
Vale Rd,
Southborough TN4 14 C1
Vale Rd, Tonbridge TN9 9 E3
Vale Rd,
Tunbridge Wells TN1 3 B4
Vale Rise TN9 9 G4
Vale Rise TN9 9 H4
Valley Dr TN11 7 E1
Valley Forge CI TN10 6 B6
Valley Mews TN6 20 D5
Valley Rd,
Crowborough TN6 20 D5
Valley Rd,
Tunbridge Wells TN413 F5
Valley Vw TN4 14 D1
Valley Vw CI TN6 20 D5
Vaughan Av TN10 6 B4
Vauxhall Gdns TN11 9 F5
Vauxhall La,
Tonbridge TN11 9 F5
Vauxhall La,
Tunbridge Wells TN411 F4
Vermont Rd TN4 13 E5
Vernon Rd TN1 15 H6
Vicarage La TN5 11 G5
Victoria Ct TN8 29 C6
Victoria Cotts,
Cranbrook TN17 27 C4
Victoria Cotts*, Victoria Rd,
Edenbridge TN8 29 C6
Victoria Rd,
Crowborough TN6 21 G6
Victoria Rd,
Edenbridge TN8 29 C6
Victoria Rd,
Mayfield TN20 23 A4
Victoria Rd,
Southborough TN4 14 A2
Victoria Rd,
Tonbridge TN11 7 E4
Victoria Rd,
Tunbridge Wells TN1 3 C1
Vines La TN11 4 B1
Vineyard La TN5 28 A4

Walters Farm Rd TN9 9 F3
Walton Rd TN10 5 G6
Warberry Park Gdns
TN4 16 B1
Ward CI TN5 19 D3
Wardsbrook Rd TN5 28 B6
Warren CI TN6 20 C4
Warren Cotts TN20 23 D4
Warren Gate TN6 20 C4
Warren Rd TN6 20 A5
Warren Ridge TN6 20 B4
Warrington Rd TN12 25 F4
Warwick Pk TN2 3 B6
Warwick Rd TN1 3 B5
Washwell La TN5 19 E4
Water La TN18 28 D2
Water Slippe TN11 7 C2
Waterdown Rd TN4 16 A4
Waterfield TN2 16 C6
Waterlakes TN8 29 C6
Waterloo Pl,
Cranbrook TN17 27 C4
Waterloo Pl,
Tonbridge TN9 9 E4
Waterloo Rd,
Cranbrook TN17 27 C3
Waterloo Rd,
Tonbridge TN9 9 E4
Watermans La TN12 25 G6
Waters Cotts TN5 19 F4
Watts CI TN5 19 E3
Watts Cross Rd TN11 4 A4
Waveney Rd TN10 5 G5
Waverley Dr TN2 15 H5
Wayside Dr TN8 29 C3
Weald Ct TN11 4 C4
Weald Vw TN5 19 F1
Weald Vw Rd TN9 9 E5
Wealden CI,
Crowborough TN6 20 D3
Wealden CI,
Tonbridge TN11 4 D5
Weare Rd TN4 15 E3
Welbeck Av TN4 15 E4
Well CI TN11 10 A2
Welland CI TN6 22 C2
Welland Rd TN10 5 G6
Weller Rd TN4 13 F5
Wellesley CI TN6 20 B5
Wellington Way TN8 29 B4
Wells CI TN10 6 A6
Welton CI TN9 8 C5
Wesley Mews TN6 20 C4
West Beeches Rd TN6 21 E4
West Park Av TN4 14 C2
West St TN20 23 A6
West Way TN6 20 C2
Westbrook Ter TN2 17 F4
Western Av TN18 28 B1
Western Gdns TN6 22 E2
Western Rd,
Cranbrook TN18 28 B1
Western Rd,
Crowborough TN6 22 D2
Western Rd,
Southborough TN4 14 C2
Western Rd,
Tunbridge Wells TN115 E6
Western Rd,
Wadhurst TN5 19 E2
Westrise TN9 8 D5
Westway TN2 18 D3
Westways TN8 29 B4
Westwood Rd,
Tonbridge TN12 26 B2
Westwood Rd,
Tunbridge Wells TN412 E4
Wheatfield CI TN17 27 B4
Wheatfield Dr TN17 27 B4
Wheatfield Lea TN17 27 B4
Wheatfield Way TN17 27 B4
Wheatsheaf Way TN10 5 H4
Whetsted Rd TN12 24 C3
Whincroft Pk TN6 20 B6
Whistler Rd TN10 6 A3
White Bear Pas TN1 3 B5
White Cottage Rd TN10 5 H4
White House Cotts
TN11 6 D4
White Oak CI TN9 9 E5
Whitebine Gdns TN12 26 C2
Whitefield Rd TN4 14 C6
Whitegate CI TN4 14 C3

Whitehill CI TN6 2
Whitehill Rd TN6 2
Whitelake Rd TN10
Whites La TN5 2
Whybourne Crest TN2 1
Wickham Gdns TN4 1
Widbury CI TN3 1
Wilderness Pk TN6 2
Willesley Gdns TN17 2
William Luck CI TN12 2
William St TN4 1
Willow Cres TN12 2
Willow Lea TN10
Willow Tree Rd TN2 1
Willow Walk TN2 1
Willowmead TN6 2
Wilman Rd TN4 1
Wilson CI TN11
Wilson Rd TN10 1
Wiltshire Way TN2 1
Winch CI TN17 2
Winchester Rd,
Cranbrook TN18 2
Winchester Rd,
Tonbridge TN10
Wincliff Rd TN9
Windmill Cotts TN17 2
Windmill La TN5 1
Windmill St TN2 1
Windsor Pl TN4 2
Windsor Rd TN6 2
Winscot CI TN6 2
Winstone Scott Av
TN3 1
Withyam Rd TN3 2
Wolfe CI TN6 2
Wolseley Rd TN4 1
Wood St TN1
Woodbury CI TN4 1
Woodbury Park Gdns
TN4 1
Woodbury Park Rd
TN4 1
Woodbury Rd TN18 2
Woodcote Rd RH18 3
Woodfield Av TN11
Woodfield Rd TN9
Woodgate Way TN9
Woodhill Pk TN4 1
Woodland CI TN4 1
Woodland Dr TN8 2
Woodland Rd TN4 1
Woodland Way,
Crowborough TN6 2
Woodland Way,
Tunbridge Wells TN41
Woodlands,
Crowborough TN6 2
Woodlands,
Tonbridge TN12 2
Woodlands,
Tunbridge Wells TN21
Woodlands Ct TN4 1
Woodlands Rd TN9
Woodpecker CI TN8 2
Woodroffe Lodge TN5 2
Woodsgate Way TN2 1
Woodside TN6 2
Woodside CI TN3 1
Woodside Rd,
Pembury TN2 1
Woodside Rd,
Tonbridge TN9
Woodside Rd,
Tunbridge Wells TN41
Woodview Cres TN11
Woolley CI TN4 1
Woolley Rd TN4 1
Wybourne Rise TN2 1
Wye Rd TN10
Wyndham Av TN11
Wyndham CI TN11 1

Yardley CI TN9
Yardley Park Rd TN9
Yeoman Gdns TN12 2
Yew Tree Rd TN4 1
York Par TN10
York Rd,
Tonbridge TN10
York Rd,
Tunbridge Wells TN1 3